Literature for Youth Series

Series Editor: Edward T. Sullivan

The Middle Ages in Literature for Youth

A Guide and Resource Book

Rebecca Barnhouse

Literature for Youth, No. 4

THE SCARECROW PRESS, INC.
Lanham, Maryland • Toronto • Oxford
2004

SCARECROW PRESS, INC.

Published in the United States of America
by Scarecrow Press, Inc.
A wholly owned subsidiary of
The Rowman & Littlefield Publishing Group, Inc.
4501 Forbes Boulevard, Suite 200, Lanham, Maryland 20706
www.scarecrowpress.com

PO Box 317
Oxford
OX2 9RU, UK

Copyright © 2004 by Rebecca Barnhouse
Cover photograph: Latin psalter, as referenced in chapter 15.

British Library Cataloguing in Publication Information Available

Library of Congress Cataloging-in-Publication Data

Barnhouse, Rebecca.
  The Middle Ages in literature for youth : a guide and resource book / Rebecca
Barnhouse.
    p. cm. — (Literature for youth ; no. 4)
  Includes bibliographical references and index.
  ISBN 0-8108-4916-X (pbk : alk. paper)
  1. Children's literature—Bibliography. 2. Young adult literature—Bibliography.
3. Middle Ages in literature—Bibliography. 4. Middle Ages—Juvenile literature—
Bibliography. I. Title. II. Literature for youth series ; no. 4.
Z6203.B35 2004
[PN1009.5.M]
011.62—dc22

                                                    2004000074

Contents

Acknowledgments

My thanks to the incomparable Chris Delfosse, without whose assistance this bibliography would never have been finished. Thanks also to the Center for Literature for Young Readers at Youngstown State University for paying Chris's wages. I also owe much to the librarians at the Public Library of Youngstown and Mahoning County and at William F. Maag Jr. Library at Youngstown State University, especially Amy Kyte and Mary Hermance, who have so enthusiastically helped me with this project. Dr. Robert Bolla, dean of arts and sciences at Youngstown State University, gave his support, for which I am thankful. And finally, my gratitude to those who have listened so patiently to my endless comments about this book, especially Nancy and Bill Barnhouse, Allison Wallace, and of course Sid Brown.

Introduction

The Middle Ages, that vast span of time from the end of the Roman Empire to the beginning of printing, can be conveniently classified as the thousand years between 500 and 1500. Less convenient is the fact that so much was going on during that millenium, from the rise of Islam to the invention of algebra, from the migrations of Germanic tribes to the supremacy of the Roman Catholic Church in Western Europe. So many cultures, so many languages and ways of life—it seems an oversimplification brought about by sheer ignorance to classify them all as "medieval." However, that is what we do, and this bibliography follows that time-honored pattern. Yet this book also attempts to combat the oversimplification of the medieval period by limiting its scope to Western Europe, for the most part, and by breaking the Middle Ages into different subjects, geographical regions, and time periods.

Historians tend to divide the thousand years into three parts, early, high, and late. The early medieval period covers approximately 500 to 1100 (or 1066 in England, when the Norman Conquest brought about large linguistic and social changes). This was a period of migration, of great kingdoms and leaders like Charlemagne and Alfred the Great, of peoples such as the Vikings, the Carolingians, and the Anglo-Saxons. The high Middle Ages, from about 1100–1300, brought with them feudalism, the rise of the universities, Gothic art and the beginnings of vernacular literature in Europe, and leaders like Eleanor of Aquitaine. "Late medieval" refers—imprecisely, of course—to the years 1300–1500, often associated with the plague and the Hundred Years' War. This time should also be remembered for great writers like Chaucer and Boccaccio, great changes in governmental systems, and great leaders, from Joan of Arc to the Lancastrian and Yorkist dynasties. The stereotyped, romanticized views of the Middle Ages in the popular imagination are most influenced by life in the high and late medieval period, when noble ladies really did wear tall pointed hats (at least, during the decades they were in fashion) and noblemen were often knights. But throughout the thousand years of the Middle Ages the vast majority of people were peasants who wore neither fancy hats nor armor of any sort.

Many of the writers whose books are included in this bibliography acknowledge the complexity of the medieval period. We are lucky that books by that doyenne of historical fiction, Rosemary Sutcliff, are still available, as are some of the works of writers of the mid-20th century like Geoffrey Trease and Cynthia Harnett, whose treatment of the later medieval period demonstrates a thorough familiarity with their subjects. Two more recent writers whose books have captured aspects of the Middle Ages admirably are Michael Cadnum, who writes convincingly about subjects as diverse as the Vikings, the Crusades, and Robin Hood, and Kevin Crossley-Holland, who has been writing about the Middle Ages for decades, and whose new Arthurian trilogy has received much-deserved praise. All of these novelists portray the medieval period responsibly, allowing their characters to be people of the Middle Ages, shaped by medieval, not modern, ideas about such concepts as class, religion, and gender.

In the past few years, several 19th-century and early 20th-century novels about Vikings and knights and battles have been reprinted, including those by G. A. Henty, the editor of *Boys Own Magazine*, whose heroic male protagonists find themselves present at decisive historical moments—and who often work with historical figures to save the day. For Henty, as for writers like Robert Louis Stevenson, Howard Pyle, and Allen French, the Middle Ages are a time of adventure and heroism, ripe for rousing action, not necessarily introspection.

Such novels may give a romanticized view of medieval life, but they can spark a reader's interest in a subject, which can be more fully explored when the novels are paired with some of the admirable nonfiction books now available, such as Cambridge University Press's Topic Books and their Introductions to History, or Lucent Publishing's World History and The Way People Live series, or Harcourt Brace's Living History series. Several writers of nonfiction and picture books deserve equal commendation. Christopher Gravett, who has worked with armor in the Tower of London, shares his considerable knowledge about knights and armor with young readers, while Kathryn Hinds brings her understanding of medieval social life to a series of books. Sheila Sancha, Joe Lasker, and Don Brown are among the picture book writers who illuminate aspects of the Middle Ages in enticing ways. Although their work may be published for elementary school readers, older students (and their teachers) could learn a great deal from their books.

I include age ranges in my descriptions of the books in this bibliography, but all of them are merely suggestions. Junior and senior high school students new to a subject will greatly increase their understanding by reading some of the impressive nonfiction titles published for elementary students, while elementary students may find just what they are looking for in books published for older readers, or ones for adults (such as Osprey Publishing's series of illustrated military histories). The age designations used here are: elementary (kindergarten through grade 3); middle (grades 4 through 6); junior (grades 7 through 9); and senior (grades 10 through 12).

This bibliography, while it makes no claim to include every book about the Middle Ages, covers both older and more recent works, some of them just published, some of them long out of print but still sitting on library shelves somewhere in America, waiting to be found by eager readers. The focus of the bibliography is on books available in the United States, although a few books from Australia, Canada, and the United Kingdom are also included. Several genres are represented here: picture books, fiction, nonfiction, reference works, and activity books. At the end of the bibliography, professional resources for educators appear; these include books, articles, and electronic resources. Finally, the last chapter offers some suggestions for classroom activities.

What this bibliography does *not* cover is the enormous number of historical fantasies published annually, books that use medieval costumes and political structures to tell stories of magic set in preindustrial neverlands. However, retellings of some medieval legends that include magic and fantastic elements are included in chapter 12—magic and the fantastic were just as much a part of the medieval imagination as they are a part of ours. Furthermore, medieval tales of the marvelous are often represented in school curricula, and these subjects—including *Beowulf*, *The Canterbury Tales*, and King Arthur—receive special attention in this bibliography.

Time-travel books also fall under the rubric of fantasy; nevertheless, I have included a few titles in which modern characters find themselves transported to the Middle Ages simply because their portrayal of some aspect of the medieval world is compelling, such as Welwyn Wilton Katz's descriptions of Viking life in *Out of the Dark*. However, in the interest of dispelling confusion, in an appendix, "Not the Middle Ages," I list some novels that are often included in bibliographies of books about the Middle Ages, but which are definitely not historical fiction.

Although the main concern of the bibliography is Western Europe, one chapter goes beyond those boundaries, describing books about Asia, the Byzantine Empire, and the Islamic world, all of which had some contact with and influence on their Western European neighbors. Yet so many books are published annually about the history of the world outside of Western Europe in the years 500–1500 that a complete bibliography would be needed to do them justice.

The books in this bibliography vary enormously in quality. I offer evaluations of them, based on my background as a medievalist, an editor, a teacher of literature, and a reader. Yet many reviewers will have opinions very different from mine. In the end, those using this bibliography will have to weigh the evidence and decide for themselves which books they want to make available to the children and teenagers with whom they work. With so many marvelous books out there, it would be hard to go too far astray!

CHAPTER ONE

Informational Books

The books in this section are not about a specific geographical region or a certain time period. Instead, they are informational books that introduce readers to aspects of the Middle Ages that cross time periods and geographical boundaries. Many are about knights and castles; a number of titles on these subjects appear every year. Other books look at the fascinating minutiae of daily life, such as food, clothing, and religious festivals. Still others cover larger political and social issues like feudalism and chivalry. Books about the plague are included in this chapter since it affected so much of Europe, even though it is associated with the 14th century.

Most of the books listed here have been well researched and present reliable information about their topics. Sometimes stereotypes and misinformation about the Middle Ages appear, and I try to alert readers to these isolated instances.

Overviews

001. Anno, Mitsumasa. *Anno's Medieval World*. 1979. Adapted from the translation by Ursula Synge. New York: Philomel, 1980. 52 pp. (0-399-20742-2 hc.) Elementary.

In his author's note, Anno says the title of his book could have been "How People Living in the Era of the Ptolemaic Theory Saw Their World," which is what he writes about here. Covering hundreds of years in a sentence, and sweeping from the early medieval period to the age of exploration, Anno focuses on the way people understood the earth and its place in the universe. His illustrations are full of fascinating details, mostly of medieval and early modern people working, and sometimes only tangentially related to the text—but you can learn just as much from them as from the text.

002. Biel, Timothy L. *The Age of Feudalism.* World History Series. San Diego: Lucent Books, 1994. 112 pp. (1-56006-232-0 lib. bdg.) Junior-Senior.

Although Biel identifies feudalism with the 11th–15th centuries, he goes back to the 5th century in Continental Europe to explain its beginnings. His focus is on the political and social structures of the feudal era, including the substantial role of the church. Inset quotations from medieval and modern sources, along with black and white reproductions of medieval and 19th-century artwork, illustrate the text. Chronology, glossary, further reading, bibliography, index.

003. Briquebec, John. *The Middle Ages: Barbarian Invasions, Empires around the World & Medieval Europe.* New York: Warwick Press, 1990. 45 pp. (0-531-19091-9 hc.) Middle-Junior.

Briquebec gives an overview not just of Western Europe, but of the entire world from 450–1450, showing the movements of peoples, the rise of religions, and the varieties of civilizations through text, paintings, and color photos. The endpapers reproduce a fascinating 1375 world map made for the king of France. Time line, glossary, index.

004. Brooks, Polly Schoyer, and Nancy Zinsses Walworth. *The World of Walls: The Middle Ages in Western Europe.* Philadelphia: J. P. Lippincott, 1966. 256 pp. Junior-Senior.

This well-written narrative history beginning with the Germanic invasions of Rome and ending with Chaucer is illustrated with black and white photos, maps, and prints. Separate chapters woven into the overarching narrative treat political, religious, and literary luminaries such as Gregory the Great, Charlemagne, Eleanor of Aquitaine, Francis of Assisi, and Chaucer. Bibliography, index.

005. Cairns, Trevor. *Barbarians, Christians, and Muslims*. Cambridge Introduction to History. Minneapolis: Lerner Publications, 1975. 100 pp. (0-8225-0803-6 lib. bdg.) Junior-Senior.
From the fall of Rome to 1066, this book discusses the lives of the Germanic people who invaded Rome, those who settled in England, and the decline and rejuvenation of the Christian church. Cairns shifts eastward to briefly cover Byzantium, Muhammad, and Islamic civilization, before looking back at Western Europe: Charlemagne, Viking incursions in England, King Alfred the Great, and finally, the Norman Conquest. This well-written history is told from a British perspective, as many of its topics, photos, and illustrations demonstrate. Index.

006. ———. *The Middle Ages*. Cambridge Introduction to World History. Cambridge: Cambridge University Press, 1972. 96 pp. (0-521-07726-5 pb.) Junior-Senior.
Cairns divides this book into chapters on the church, the feudal lords, "Religion and the Warriors," which covers the Crusades, "The Ordinary People," which looks at rural and urban life as well as trade, "Kings and Countries," and finally "The End of the Middle Ages." Like other books in this series, this one is thorough and accurate and illustrated with well-chosen photos and drawings. The time line is divided into four parts, showing what was going on simultaneously with the church, the feudal lords, the ordinary people, and in countries other than England.

007. Caselli, Giovanni. *The Middle Ages*. History of Everyday Things Series. 1988. New York: Peter Bedrick, 1991. 48 pp. (0-87226-176-X hc.) Middle.
Four-page chapters on topics like "Knights and the Crusades," "The Venice of Marco Polo," and "Entertainments and Tournaments" contain plenty of illustrations with captions, along with a short amount of text. Many of the appealing colored drawings are based on manuscript illuminations. Readers will be introduced to rural, urban, and castle life in the high and late Middle Ages, as well as to crafts, trade, and medicine. Bibliography.

008. ———. *The Roman Empire and the Dark Ages*. History of Everyday Things Series. New York: Peter Bedrick Books, 1985. 48 pp. (0-911745-58-0 hc.) Elementary-Middle.

Caselli attempts to give a history of material culture, of "people through the things that they made," from 50 BCE to 1300 CE. Each four-page chapter is packed with text and numbered illustrations, each with a caption (e.g., "A claw hammer," or "Heads of battle axes"). Subjects include: a Celtic farmer, a Roman villa, Roman town life, Vindolanda (the Roman fortress in England) in 150 CE, the Anglo-Saxons, Byzantium, the Arabs in Europe ca. 800, the Vikings, and life in medieval European castles, monasteries, and towns. For each subject, we see clothing, writing, tools, jewelry, architecture, cooking utensils, and maps. Chronology, further reading.

009. Corrick, James A. *The Early Middle Ages*. World History Series. San Diego: Lucent Books, 1995. 128 pp. (1-56006-246-0 lib bdg.) Junior.

Defining the time period as the fourth to the tenth centuries, Corrick covers all of Europe, including the Franks in the West, Byzantium in the East, Islam in Spain, and the Vikings in Scandinavia. Although his scope is vast, by keeping his focus on political and religious institutions, he ably introduces many important subjects, from Christian monasticism and its role in the transmission of learning, to the origins of feudalism and the rights of serfs. Quotations from important medieval documents enhance the text. The one weakness of this book—and this series—is the use of illustrations from 19th-century engravings (unidentified as such), which present romanticized views of the Middle Ages. Glossary, bibliography, further reading, index.

010. ———. *The Late Middle Ages*. San Diego: Lucent Books, 1995. 112 pp. (1-56006-279-7 lib. bdg.) Junior.

Carrying on from where he left off in the last book, Corrick covers the political history of the 11th–15th centuries, breaking each chapter into a different geographical region: Norman England, Capetian France, the Holy Roman Empire in Germany and Italy, and the Byzantine Empire. Another chapter is devoted to the Crusades. Paragraph-long overviews of important rulers appear within the chapters, and inset quotations, along with black and white illustrations, are used. Glossary, bibliography, further reading, index.

011. Dambrosio, Monica, and Roberto Barbieri. *History of the World: The Early Middle Ages.* Translation of *Splendore barbarico.* 1989. Austin, TX: Steck-Vaughn, 1992. 72 pp. Junior.

Double-page spreads with a considerable amount of text illustrated by paintings and maps focus on the political and religious history of Eastern and Western Europe, North Africa, and the Middle East from the fifth through the tenth centuries. Early Christianity and the rise of Islam are covered. Despite numerous large illustrations which make the book appear to be designed for younger readers, the complicated text, which includes concepts like Arianism and other heresies, anchoritic versus cenobitic monasticism, and iconoclasm, seems aimed at a junior high or older audience. Glossary, index.

012. ———. *History of the World: The Late Middle Ages.* Translation of *Dentro il Medioevo.* 1989. Austin, TX: Steck-Vaughn, 1992. 72 pp. (0-8172-3308-3 lib. bdg.) Junior.

Focusing on economy, trade, and religion in Eastern and Western Europe from 1000–1300, this volume, like the previous one, contains maps and paintings. Also like the previous volume, this one includes complex information about religious and political controversies, like the Great Schism. The Continental emphasis makes this a valuable volume for collections with a concentration on works about the British Isles. Glossary, index.

013. Deary, Terry. *Measly Middle Ages.* Illus. Martin Brown. Horrible Histories Series. New York: Scholastic, 1998. 128 pp. (0-590-49848-7 pb.) Elementary-Middle.

Using comics, humor, and gross facts, Deary presents a simplistic but entertaining introduction to the Middle Ages. "Gruesome games [and] revolting recipes" are included.

014. Gregory, Tony. *The Dark Ages.* The Illustrated History of the World Series. New York: Facts on File, 1991. 80 pp. (0-8160-2787-0 hc.) Middle-Junior.

From the 3rd to the 11th centuries in Europe, Asia, the Americas, Africa, and the Pacific, this book gives an overview of cultures, migrations, religions, and peoples. The first half concentrates on Western Europe, covering it in more detail, leaving two pages for all of India and

Southeast Asia, four for China, two for Africa, etc. Color maps, paintings, and photos are included on every page. Time line, glossary, index, further reading.

015. Hanawalt, Barbara A. *The Middle Ages: An Illustrated History*. New York: Oxford University Press, 1998. 160 pp. (0-19-510359-9 hc.) Junior-Senior.

This impressive overview by a renowned medieval historian shows both the large historical events and the fascinating details of daily life. Carefully chosen examples, quotations, and color photos in the insets enhance the text, which tells about the variety of cultures important to the period 500–1500: Roman, Germanic, Christian, and Arab. Chronology, glossary, further reading, index.

016. Hart, Avery, and Paul Mantell. *Knights and Castles: 50 Hands-On Activities to Experience the Middle Ages*. Illus. Michael Kline. Charlotte, VT: Williamson Publishing, 1998. 96 pp. (1-885593-17-1 pb.) Elementary.

By trying to cover so much material, the authors vastly oversimplify much of the information they present, leading to stereotypes and inaccuracies: for example, Charlemagne was hardly a "tribal warlord" who wore "animal skins instead of cloth," as they portray him, and the word histories they present often owe more to the imagination than to etymology. Readers will come away from this book with a simplistic, negative understanding of the medieval period. However, teachers will appreciate the "Then and Now" questions, which ask students to think about social systems, laws, and other conventions in their own lives. Activities include games like Hunt the Slipper, recipes, art projects, a short play about St. George and the Dragon, and writing projects. Bibliography, index.

017. Howarth, Sarah. *The Middle Ages*. See Through History Series. New York: Viking, 1993. 48 pp. (0-670-85098-5 hc.) Elementary.

The four "see-through scenes," in which a page of plastic is laid over another page—lift it to see the people inside the building—is the only feature distinguishing this series from others. Double-page spreads, one per topic, have several paragraphs of text illustrated with paintings and photos. The focus is on life in Western Europe in the later Middle Ages. Chronology, glossary.

018. León, Vicki. *Outrageous Women of the Middle Ages*. New York: John Wiley and Sons, 1998. 128 pp. (0-471-17004-6 pb.) Middle-Junior.
Like León's *Uppity Women* series for adults, this book uses humor, playful language, and fascinating facts to hook readers. The 14 women she writes about in this volume lived between the 6th and 14th centuries in Europe, Asia, and Africa. Some, like Eleanor of Aquitaine and Clare of Assisi, are well known, while readers may never have heard of others, like Sonduk of Korea. But all of them did something impressive before they reached the age of 20. Black and white illustrations, time line, further reading.

019. Macdonald, Fiona. *First Facts about the Middle Ages*. Created and designed by David Salariya. New York: Peter Bedrick Books, 1997. 31 pp. (0-97226-533-1 lib. bdg.) Elementary.
Charming colored drawings illustrate each double-page spread, which begins with a fact like "Twelve-year-olds could get married" and is then crammed with other tidbits about life in the late medieval period, with an emphasis on the negative parts. The short glossary seems almost unrelated to the text.

020. ———. *The Middle Ages*. Everyday Life Series. Morristown, NJ: Silver Burdett, 1987. 61 pp. (0-382-06833-5 hc.) Elementary.
The lives of ordinary Europeans of all classes from 1200–1500 are portrayed in paintings, color reproductions of medieval art, and photos. In 25 two-page chapters, Macdonald introduces concepts like feudalism, and tells about pilgrimages, town life, castles, and trade. Because of the brevity of her text, she can only provide the most general of information. Chronology, glossary, index.

021. ———. *Women in Medieval Times*. The Other Half of History Series. New York: Peter Bedrick, 2000. 48 pp. (0-87226-569-2 lib. bdg.) Elementary.
Because she has to cover all of Europe from 1000–1500, Macdonald can't give much space to any one topic. For example, women's education receives a single paragraph. Nevertheless, the range of subjects is impressive, and the viewpoint broad enough to encompass both sides of vexed issues—we read not just about the dowry a bride's family provided, but

the dower a husband's family promised to the bride, should her husband die. Good color reproductions of medieval artwork appear on every page, as do interesting inset quotations. Glossary, further reading, index.

022. *The Middle Ages*. (No author.) London: Marshall Cavendish, 1995. 64 pp. (1-85435-856-1 hc.) Middle.

Focusing on William I, Richard I, and King John, the book provides biographical information about each before mentioning achievements from that ruler's time. Two of the sections also include a story, one narrated by a monk who is in the Holy Land for the Crusades, and one told by a peasant boy on an English manor. Photos, paintings, and reproductions of medieval art compete with the text for space in these very crowded pages. Glossary, chronology, bibliography, index.

023. Morris, Neil, John Malam, and Anne McRae. *The Atlas of the Medieval World in Europe (IV–XV Century)*. New York: Peter Bedrick, 1999. 62 pp. (0-87226-530-7 hc.) Middle.

Large, double-page spreads, each covering a topic like "The Crusades" or "The Growth of Towns" or "The Mongol Empire," are crammed with illustrations, both paintings and photos. Each topic gets a short, main paragraph, but the majority of text is in the sometimes lengthy picture captions. Index.

024. Oakes, Catherine. *Exploring the Past: The Middle Ages*. Illus. Stephen Biesty. San Diego: Harcourt Brace Jovanovich, 1989. 64 pp. (0-512-00451-3 hc.) Elementary-Middle.

In this large-format book each new section—"The Arts and Learning," "Religion," "Life of the Nobility," "Life in the Country," "Life in the Towns," and "The Wider World"—begins with a double-page color painting filled with fascinating details of an illuminator's workshop or life in an abbey of a castle under siege. Many of the illustrations were inspired by medieval art. This is a good introduction to the high and late Middle Ages in Western Europe. Time line, index.

025. Ormrod, Mark. *Life in the Middle Ages*. Themes in History Series. East Sussex, England: Wayland, 1991. 48 pp. (0-7502-0237-8 lib. bdg.) Elementary.

With its color photos of medieval art and architecture and its coverage of unusual material, this volume stands out from similar titles. It focuses on the years 1000–1500 and briefly discusses modern conceptions about the Middle Ages before giving an overview of the medieval period. Inset paragraphs and illustrations cover topics such as telling time, the work of serfs, the layout of an abbey, and the cloth trade in England. The last chapter looks at survivals and influences of the Middle Ages—ideas, artistic styles, and languages, for example. Time line, glossary, further reading, index.

026. Rice, Earle, Jr. *Life During the Middle Ages.* The Way People Live Series. San Diego: Lucent Books, 1998. 96 pp. (1-560-06386-6 hc.) Junior-Senior.

A thousand years in 96 pages! The unsuccessful handling of such a broad scope makes this one of the least impressive titles in this otherwise admirable series. Rice includes too much extraneous information and relies far too heavily on long quotations from modern sources, many of which are too difficult for the intended audience. He takes a textbook approach, listing, for example, "The Six Key Elements of Feudalism," as he tackles social and economic structures, art, science, education, religion, and daily life. Some interesting features of rural and urban life during the high and late Middle Ages emerge, but we learn little about life during the early Middle Ages. Glossary, chronology.

Daily Life

027. Aliki. *A Medieval Feast.* New York: Crowell, 1983. 32 pp. (0-690-04245-0 hc.) Elementary.

Enticing illustrations based on medieval artwork will draw readers into the story of the preparations needed when the king announces that he will visit a manor house. The lord and lady of the manor, as well as all the servants and the people in the village, work hard to prepare the feast with which the book ends. Author's note.

028. Beckett, Wendy. *The Duke and the Peasant: Life in the Middle Ages.* Munich and New York: Prestel-Verlag, 1997. 32 pp. (3-7913-1813-6 hc.) Elementary.

The calendar pictures in the Limbourg brothers' 15th-century book of hours, the *Très Riches Heures*, are reproduced, illustrating the lives of both peasants and nobles. A paragraph of text tells us what to look for in each picture.

029. Black, Irma Simonton. *Castle, Abbey and Town: How People Lived in the Middle Ages.* Illus. W. T. Mars. New York: Holiday House, 1963. 101 pp. Middle.

Appealing black and white pencil sketches accompany the solid textual introduction to life in a medieval castle, within the church, and in a town in the high Middle Ages. Interspersed within the nonfiction sections are interrelated stories about the people who might have lived in and around the castle. There are some inaccuracies—like the assertion that "a real King Arthur probably met with his Knights of the Round Table" in sixth-century England.

030. Clare, John D. *Medieval Towns.* I Was There Series. London: Bodley Head, 1992. 64 pp. (0-370-31746-7 hc.) Elementary-Middle.

fourteenth-century Europe literally comes alive in fascinating photos of reenactors in medieval settings. Adopted for the British National Curriculum, this book is carefully researched and ends with a discussion about the complexity of sources for medieval history. It presents a pessimistic view of the 14th century, showing many scenes of dirt and violence, sickness and death. Two or three paragraphs are given to each topic, such as apprenticeship, schools, farming and famine, and rebellions. Chronology, index.

031. Cosman, Madeleine Pelner. *Medieval Holidays and Festivals: A Calendar of Celebrations.* New York: Scribner's, 1981. 136 pp. (0-684-17172-4 hc.) Junior-Senior.

Pelner, who has been the director of the Institute for Medieval and Renaissance Studies at the City College of the City University of New York, focuses on 12 medieval holidays, one for each month, explaining customs, games, food, plays, and songs associated with each. She includes one chapter of recipes and another giving instructions for making decorations. Groups planning a medieval feast or festival will find this book particularly useful. Further reading, index.

032. Dawson, Imogen. *Clothes and Crafts in the Middle Ages.* 1997. Milwaukee: Gareth Stevens Publishing, 2000. 32 pp. (0-8368-2736-8 hc.) Elementary-Middle.

Despite its title, this book introduces readers to many medieval topics, from pilgrimages to feasts. Although it mentions crafts, it contains little detail about them. Many of the photos are taken from early modern, not medieval, works. Instructions about how to make a kirtle, tunic, aluminum foil chain, coat of arms, pilgrim's badge, and an illuminated manuscript are included. Glossary, index, further reading.

033. ———. *Food and Feasts in the Middle Ages*. New Discovery Books. New York: Macmillan, 1994. 32 pp. (0-02-726324-X hc.) Elementary-Middle.
Fascinating information about what people of all classes ate in the later Middle Ages is supplemented by photographs from medieval manuscripts and inset quotations from medieval texts about table manners, recipes, and menus. Recipes for thick leek soup, pease porridge, lamb stew, and "Honey toast with pine nuts" are included, making this a useful book for any age group interested in cooking a medieval meal. Glossary, further reading, index.

034. Hartman, Gertrude. *Medieval Days and Ways*. 1937. New York: Macmillan, 1965. 332 pp. Junior-Senior.
Although dated by both its patronizing tone and some of the information it presents, this book still has some good material about the high and late medieval periods. Into her descriptions of castle, town, and country life Hartman weaves interesting quotations from medieval texts, such as the notes scribes sometimes wrote at the end of the manuscripts they had copied, complaining of their weariness. Black and white illustrations are sprinkled throughout the text, which ends with a chapter on the legacy of the Middle Ages in the United States. Index.

035. Hinds, Kathryn. *Life in the Middle Ages: The Castle*. Benchmark Books. Tarrytown, New York: Marshall Cavendish, 2001. 80 pp. (0-761-41007-4 lib. bdg.) Middle.
Hinds's text is as beautifully written as it is illustrated, with full-color images from medieval manuscripts and tapestries. The focus is 1100–1400, but a quick overview of the entire medieval period begins the book. Lists of further reading and on line information, as well as quotations from medieval texts, supplement chapters about the ways men, women, and children lived in European castles. The other books in Hinds's series,

following, follow the same format and are of equally high quality. Each includes descriptions of pilgrims from Chaucer's *The Canterbury Tales*.

036. ———. *Life in the Middle Ages: The Church*. Benchmark Books. Tarrytown, New York: Marshall Cavendish, 2001. 80 pp. (0-7614-1008-2 lib. bdg.) Middle.

This volume includes information on both Christians and non-Christians, as well as visual and verbal portraits of appropriate pilgrims from the General Prologue of *The Canterbury Tales*, in this case, the Prioress, Monk, and Friar.

037. ———. *Life in the Middle Ages: The City*. Benchmark Books. Tarrytown, New York: Marshall Cavendish, 2001. 80 pp. (0-7614-1005-8 lib. bdg.) Middle.

Readers will learn about trades and guilds, growing up in a city, games and songs, even how large different cities were. Like the other volumes in this series, this one is packed with fascinating information.

038. ———. *Life in the Middle Ages: The Countryside*. Benchmark Books. Tarrytown, New York: Marshall Cavendish, 2001. 80 pp. (0-7614-1006-4 lib. bdg.) Middle.

"In the Middle Ages, very few people believed in any sort of equality." From the first sentence of chapter 1, Hinds makes it clear how different the European Middle Ages were from modern America, especially in terms of social class. In words and illustrations, she shows the lives of both the nobility and the peasantry on European manors of the later medieval period.

039. Howarth, Sarah. *Medieval People*. Brookfield, CT: Millbrook Press, 1992. 48 pp. (1-56294-153-4 lib. bdg.) Elementary-Middle.

Using illustrations from medieval art and quotations from medieval texts, Howarth describes 13 types from the later Middle Ages: chronicler, king, pope, bishop, knight, pilgrim, lady, herald, monk, doctor, heretic, mason, and merchant. This book would make a good companion to the General Prologue of *The Canterbury Tales*. Glossary, further reading, index.

040. ———. *Medieval Places*. Brookfield, CT: Millbrook Press, 1991. 48 pp. (1-56294-152-6 lib. bdg.) Elementary-Middle.

Like the previous volume, this one uses medieval quotations and illustrations, this time to present physical places, and the ideas attached to them, from the high and late medieval period. One strength of this book is its inclusion of some places rarely dealt with in other books, like the guildhall and the parish church. Other subjects are the field, the peasant's cottage, the castle, the battlefield, the forest, the law court, the school, the university, the road, the port, and the market. Glossary, further reading, index.

041. Langley, Andrew. *Medieval Life*. Photos by Geoff Brightling and Geoff Dann. Dorling Kindersley Eyewitness Books. New York: Knopf, 1996. 64 pp. (0-7894-6038-6 hc.) Elementary-Middle-Junior.
Like other books in the Eyewitness series, this one uses appealing photos of artifacts and reproductions of period art, each with its own short caption. Clothing, beds, spoons and table knives, shields, weapons, jewelry, tools, beehives, quill pens and inkwells, pilgrims' badges, musical instruments, coins, charters—the inclusion of fascinating details from all classes of society makes this a book to pore over. Index.

042. Lasker, Joe, writer/illus. *Merry Ever After: The Story of Two Medieval Weddings*. New York: Viking, 1976. 48 pp. (0-670-47257-3 hc.) Elementary.
Delightful illustrations inspired by late medieval artists (including Dürer, the Limbourg brothers, Brueghel, Roger van der Weyden, and anonymous artists of books of hours) tell the parallel stories of a noble and a peasant wedding, both decided on by the couples' fathers. None of the teenagers are asked what they think of the arrangements, and none of them are surprised or upset, as modern teens might be. The only inaccuracy is the implication that all medieval people married at 14 or 15; in reality peasants usually married in their later teens or early 20s. Nevertheless, this is a wonderful book.

043. Macdonald, Fiona. *How Would You Survive in the Middle Ages?* Illus. Mark Peppe. New York: Franklin Watts, 1995. 48 pp. (0-531-14343-0 lib. bdg.) Middle.
Asking questions to prompt readers to think about what is happening in the pictures, the book is dense with pictorial and textual details about life in medieval towns and castles, as well as in the countryside.

044. ———. *You Wouldn't Want to Be in a Medieval Dungeon! Prisoners You'd Rather Not Meet.* Illus. David Antram. New York: Franklin Watts, 2003. 32 pp. (0-531-16651-1 pb.) Elementary.

Life in a medieval dungeon—criminals, rats and lice, the wrongly jailed, punishments—as told by the jailer in a 15th-century prison. Index.

045. McGovern, Ann. *If You Lived in the Days of the Knights.* If You Lived Series. Illus. Dan Andreasen. New York: Scholastic, 2001. 80 pp. (0-439-10565-X pb.) Middle.

Using a question-answer format, McGovern introduces readers to life in England in the year 1250: clothing, food, castle life, knights, peasants.

046. Morgan, Gwyneth. *Life in a Medieval Village.* A Cambridge Topic Book. 1975. Minneapolis: Lerner, 1982. 52 pp. (0-8225-1207-6 lib. bdg.) Junior-Senior.

Morgan takes as her subject the 13th-century English village owned by Lord Robert Fitzralph—the lives and work of serfs and nobles, the social hierarchy, the role of Christianity, law and judgment. Readers who want specific details about spinning, or peasants' clothing, or the difference between free and unfree peasants, or a female peasant's duties, will find them here, illustrated by black and white photos and reproductions of medieval art. Like other books in this series, Morgan's is carefully researched and demonstrates a deep understanding of medieval social life. Index.

047. Nikola-Lisa, W. *Till Year's Good End: A Calendar of Medieval Labors.* Illus. Christopher Manson. New York: Atheneum, 1997. 32 pp. (0-689-80020-7 hc.) Elementary.

Each double-page spread has a rhyming couplet at the top indicating the work of the month, which is explained in more detail in the text at the bottom of the page. Charming illustrations, based on those in early printed books, place the events in the high or late medieval period.

048. Sancha, Sheila. *The Luttrell Village: Country Life in the Middle Ages.* New York: Thomas Y. Crowell, 1982. 64 pp. (0-690-04324-4 lib. bdg.) Elementary.

Using the famous 14th-century illuminated Luttrell Psalter (which is on display in the British Library in London) as an inspiration for her illustrations, Sancha gives us an agricultural year in an English village in this wonderful book.

049. ———. *Walter Dragun's Town: Crafts and Trade in the Middle Ages.* New York: Thomas Y. Crowell, 1987. 64 pp. (0-690-04804-1 hc.) Elementary.

Using medieval records, Sancha re-creates the town of Stanford, England, in 1274. Readers learn, in fascinating visual and written detail, about cloth, leather, and metal making, village, castle, and religious life (one fourth of the town's inhabitants were in holy orders), and the middle class's difficulty with the ruling gentry and nobility. This is one of the best introductions to medieval town life, and although it's marketed for younger readers, all ages can learn from it. Glossary.

050. Sichel, Marion, writer/illus. *Costume Reference 1: Roman Britain and the Middle Ages.* Boston: Plays, 1977. 72 pp. (0-8238-0211-6 hc.) Junior-Senior.

A former theatrical costume designer discusses clothing styles, including hair, head coverings, shoes, jewelry, and styles worn by different classes from the end of Roman Britain through the late medieval period. She includes the often-neglected back views of clothes in her drawings. Despite a very few misrepresentations, this is an indispensable book for anyone who wants details about medieval clothing. Glossary, bibliography, index.

051. Wroble, Lisa A. *Kids in the Middle Ages.* Kids throughout History Series. New York: Powerkids Press, 2001. 24 pp. (0-823-95120-0 lib. bdg.) Elementary.

Simon, a peasant boy who lives in a village, is the focus as readers learn about medieval life and death in short chapters covering topics like the plague, farming, and life in a village. Reproductions of 16th-century, not medieval, artwork are used as illustrations, and there are a few inaccuracies in the text.

Knights and Chivalry

052. Buehr, Walter, writer/illus. *Chivalry and the Mailed Knights.* New York: Putnam's, 1963. 94 pp. Middle.

Two-color pencil sketches illustrate this informational book about 12th- to 15th-century knights. The elements of heraldry are covered, as are a knight's training, life, weapons, and armor, in chapters of six to eight pages of continuous text. Buehr wrote several other books about the medieval period, including *The Crusades* and *Knights and Castles and Feudal Life*. Glossary, index.

053. Cairns, Trevor. *Medieval Knights*. Cambridge Introduction to World History. Cambridge: Cambridge University Press, 1992. 64 pp. (0-521-38953-4 pb.) Middle-Junior-Senior.

Going back to the end of the Roman Empire, Cairns traces the development of medieval knighthood, distinguishing between professional and non-professional soldiers, and discussing the influence of Christianity on knighthood. Readers get a short history of medieval Europe, including Byzantium, Islam, and the rise of feudalism. Women's roles, the poetry of chivalry, heraldry, the knighting ritual, and a wealth of other information are illustrated with black and white photos, drawings, and artwork, as well as with substantial quotations from medieval sources. This is a careful, authoritative work for strong readers who already know a little about knights.

054. Carlson, Laurie. *Days of Knights and Damsels: An Activity Guide*. Chicago: Chicago Review Press, 1998. 184 pp. (1-556-52291-6 pb.) Elementary.

Over 100 illustrated projects, recipes, and games, some only marginally connected to the Middle Ages, are included here: food, clothing (a "princess hat"), calligraphy, printing, geometry, crocheting—the list goes on. The book's strength is its activities, not its portrayal of the medieval period, which is generic and sometimes dependent on stereotypes.

055. Chorzempa, Rosemary A. *Design Your Own Coat of Arms: An Introduction to Heraldry*. New York: Dover, 1987. 48 pp. (0-486-24993-X pb.) Middle-Adult.

Line drawings accompany the text, which explains the elements of heraldry.

056. Clare, John D. *Knights in Armor*. Living History Series. New York: Harcourt Brace Jovanovich, 1992. 64 pp. (0-15-200508-0 hc.) Elementary-Middle.

This series uses photos of costumed actors as illustrations for the several paragraphs of text per double-page spread. A valuable part of this book is its step-by-step photos of the arming of a knight. Hunting, the education of a knight, the tournament, and the roles of women are also covered. Index.

057. Corbin, Carole Lynn. *Knights*. New York: Franklin Watts, 1989. 64 pp. (0-531-10692-6 lib. bdg.) Elementary.

The introduction, with its references to 80s television shows, dates this book, and the prose is far from distinguished. However, the color illustrations, many of them reproductions of medieval art, are appealing and well-chosen. A knight's training and life, as well as life for others inside a castle, are the subjects. Further reading, index.

058. Corrick, James A. *Life of a Medieval Knight*. The Way People Live Series. San Diego: Lucent Books, 2001. 96 pp. (1-560-06817-5 lib. bdg.) Middle-Junior-Senior.

Corrick's work is so filled with information, including many quotations and illustrations from medieval sources, that it could serve as a general study of knighthood for students from sixth grade through college. It includes the expected information about chivalry, feudalism, and the Crusades, but also topics like "The Weakness of Mail" and "The Death of Horses." Although each section is short, each is packed with fascinating information. Many of the books in the useful annotated further reading list are appropriate for adults, not children.

059. Daly-Weir, Catherine. *Coat of Arms*. Illus. Jeff Crosby. New York: Grosset and Dunlap, 2000. 32 pp. (0-448-41975-0 pb.) Elementary.

This introduction to heraldry includes full-color paintings of late medieval knights and a simple text explaining the elements of heraldry. A plastic stencil to help readers create designs for their own coats of arms comes with the book.

060. Farman, John. *The Short and Bloody History of Knights*. Short and Bloody History Series. Mineapolis: Lerner, 2002. 96 pp. (0-822-50842-7 pb.) Junior.

Using humorous prose and pen-and-ink drawings, Farman covers the history of knighthood, armor and weapons, the Crusades, and castles. Glossary, index, further reading.

061. Fradon, Dana. *Sir Dana: A Knight; As Told by His Trusty Armor*. New York: Dutton, 1988. 40 pp. (0-525-44424-6 lib. bdg.) Elementary.

A *New Yorker* cartoonist teaches young readers about knights by having a suit of armor in a modern museum tell a group of schoolchildren about the knight who wore it. The book is illustrated with color cartoons.

062. Gibbons, Gail. *Knights in Shining Armor.* Boston: Little, Brown, 1995. 32 pp. (0-316-30948-6 hc.) Elementary.

Charming pen, watercolor, and colored pencil illustrations accompany an informative text introducing readers to knights—where they lived, what they wore, how they dressed and spent their time, what weapons they carried, and how a boy became a knight.

063. Gibson, Michael. *The Knights.* The Living Past Series. New York: Arco Publishing, 1984. 61 pp. (0-688-04785-2 lib. bdg.) Middle-Junior.

Color paintings and photos of medieval artwork accompany the text, which focuses on warfare in the high and late Middle Ages, and particularly the Crusades. Each subject—the squire, the tournament, the Battle of Crécy—gets a double-page spread with text and illustration. "A Chronicle of the Crusades" usefully defines each of the nine crusades in a paragraph. Time line, index.

064. Glubok, Shirley. *Knights in Armor.* New York: Harper and Row, 1969. 48 pp. Elementary.

Relying on black and white photos of armor from museums and reproductions of medieval art as illustrations, Glubok explains how boys became pages, then squires, and finally knights. She describes the parts and different styles of armor and weapons, and then discusses the Arthurian legend.

065. Gravett, Christopher. *Knight.* Photos by Geoff Dann. Dorling Kindersley Eyewitness Books. New York: Knopf, 1993. 64 pp. (0-679-83882-1 hc.) Elementary-Middle-Junior.

This book gives an impressive overview of its topic through a skillful placement of text and illustration. Photos of armor and weapons from different time periods and different European countries accompany a history of knights. Both peacetime and wartime activities of knights, including the Crusades, are discussed, and readers witness a squire arming a knight in step-by-step photos. Gravett, who has an M.A. in medieval studies, has worked in both the British Museum and the Royal Armouries in the Tower of London. Index.

066. ———. *The Knight's Handbook: How to Become a Knight in Shining Armor*. New York: Cobblehill, 1997. 36 pp. (0-525-65241-8 hc.) Middle.
In addition to excellent photos and a text explaining the steps to knighthood (and the basic ideas associated with chivalry, such as armor, weapons, heraldry, the Crusades, and castle life), Gravett includes activities associated with each topic. Readers get detailed instructions for making helmets, swords, castles, shields, even catapults. Some recipes are also included.

067. ———. *The World of the Medieval Knight*. Illus. Brett Breckon. New York: Peter Bedrick Books, 1996. 64 pp. (0-87226-277-4 hc.) Elementary-Middle.
Twenty-seven topics, from the castle to seige warfare to ladies, with a focus on warfare and armor of the later medieval period, are each dealt with in a double-page spread with several paintings, a central paragraph, and several shorter paragraph-length captions. Glossary, index.

068. Lasker, Joe, writer/illus. *A Tournament of Knights*. New York: Thomas Y. Crowell, 1986. 32 pp. (0-690-04541-7 hc.) Elementary.
Lasker uses the story of a young knight's first tournament to introduce the idea of jousting. Readers will learn as much about late medieval court life from his sumptuous, historically accurate illustrations as they will from the text. Glossary.

069. Matthews, John. *The Barefoot Book of Knights*. Illus. Giovanni Manna. Cambridge, MA: Barefoot Books, 2002. 80 pp. (1-841-48064-9 lib. bdg.) Elementary-Middle.
Matthews uses an odd and not completely successful combination of techniques to introduce knights and chivalry. He gives historical information about knights, then presents a ten-year-old boy who is training to be a knight. Instead of following through with a story about Tom, however, Tom learns through stories of famous knights (Matthews gives the sources for them). A compact disc version is also available.

070. Nicolle, David. *Medieval Knights*. See Through History Series. New York: Viking, 1997. 48 pp. (0-670-87463-9 hc.) Middle.

Double-page spreads combine paintings, photos, and a substantial amount of text to cover subjects such as heraldry, the feudal system, medicine, Crusades, and clothing. Chronology, glossary, index.

071. O'Brien, Patrick. *The Making of a Knight: How Sir James Earned His Armor.* Watertown, MA: Charlesbridge, 1998. 32 pp. (0-881-06355-X hc.) Elementary.

In 15th-century England, a 7-year-old boy becomes a page, then a squire at age 14, and finally, at 21, a knight. Full-page oil paintings and smaller inset pictures show details about castle life.

072. Osprey Publishing (Oxford, England) puts out a huge number of short but authoritative books on all aspects of military history. Although the books are published for adults, they are accessible to readers in middle grades and above.

The books are usually 48 or 64 pages long and illustrated with color plates. Subjects include the Normans, the Battle of Hastings, Agincourt, the age of Charlemagne, tournaments, and medieval siege warfare. Some books are much more specific, such as Christopher Gravett's *English Medieval Knight 1400–1500* and *German Medieval Armies 1300–1500* or Ian Heath's *Byzantine Armies 1118–1461.* A few of their titles are included within the appropriate sections of this bibliography. For lists of Osprey's books consult their website at www.ospreypublishing.com.

073. Steele, Philip. *Knights.* New York: Kingfisher, 1998. 64 pp. (0-753-45154-9 hc.) Elementary-Middle.

Heraldry, armor, jousts, horses, weapons; in short, all about knights, with plenty of illustrations. Steele includes sections about "knights" of other cultures (Japanese samurai and Sioux warriors, for example), and portrayals of knights in modern movies. Glossary, index.

074. Windrow, Martin. *The Medieval Knight.* Illus. Richard Hook. The Soldier through the Ages Series. New York: Franklin Watts, 1985. 32 pp. (0-531-03834-8 hc.) Elementary-Middle.

The training and life of late medieval knights is told here, accompanied by full-page paintings. Windrow keeps his focus on military history: how knights fought, what weapons brought about the downfall of knights, how knights earned money. Glossary, time line, index.

075. Wright, Rachel. *Knights: Facts, Things to Make, Activities.* Craft Topics Series. New York: Franklin Watts, 1991. 32 pp. (0-531-14163-2 lib. bdg.) Elementary.
Color photos, paintings, and medieval art illustrate the sections of this book that introduce readers to knights and armor. Interspersed with these sections are activities with step-by-step photos and instructions (including making a cardboard knight's helmet, a stained-glass window, a miniature jousting scene, and a castle). Glossary, further reading, index.

076. Yue, Charlotte, and David Yue. *Armor.* New York: Houghton Mifflin, 1994. 92 pp. (0-395-68101-4 hc.) Middle-Junior-Senior.
Fascinating pencil sketches illustrate the well-written text in this handsome volume. The history and development of armor, the intricacies of its construction, the work of the armorer, and the elements of heraldry are discussed, and the last chapter briefly covers armor from cultures outside of Western Europe. The reader who wants to truly understand armor won't want to miss this book. Bibliography, index.

077. Zohorsky, Janet R. *Medieval Knights and Warriors.* History Makers Series. San Diego: Lucent Books, 2002. 112 pp. (1-560-06954-6 lib. bdg.) Middle-Junior.
After a chapter describing the world of the medieval knight, Zohorsky focuses on six warriors, each in his own chapter: William Marshal, Richard the Lionheart, Saladin, Don Pero Nino, Bertrand du Guesclin, and Sir John de Hawkwood, a mercenary. Further reading, bibliography, index.

Castles

078. Biesty, Stephen. *Stephen Biesty's Cross Sections: Castle.* Written by Richard Platt. New York: Dorling Kindersley, 1994. 32 pp. (1-56458-467-4 hc.) Elementary.
This large-format volume about a 14th-century English castle, with the characteristic Dorling Kindersley double-page spreads packed with detailed annotated pictures and varieties of type sizes, has a hook: in each picture, a spy is hidden (à la Hilary Knight's *Where's Wallace?*) and readers have to search to find him. The cutaway illustrations of the castle

show all levels of society and all levels of activity, from people sitting on latrines to men putting out a roof fire. This busy book will appeal to readers who like to lose themselves in the details, especially gory ones like methods of torture or gong farming. Glossary, index.

079. Blackwood, Gary L. *Life in a Medieval Castle*. The Way People Live Series. San Diego: Lucent Books, 2000. 108 pp. (1-560-06582-6 lib. bdg.) Middle-Junior-Senior.

After a short overview of feudalism, Blackwood turns to a discussion of the history and varieties of castles, and then to the kinds of people who inhabited them. Readers learn about the castle builders, the blacksmiths, the squires and attendants, and the castle's lord and his family. Filled with intriguing information about the lives of the nobility, including sanitation and health, what people ate and when, how they entertained themselves, how children were educated, and how knights fought, the book also delves into the lives of the lower classes who kept a castle running. This impressive volume focuses on the high and late Middle Ages.

080. Brochard, P. *Castles of the Middle Ages*. New York: Silver Burdett, 1985. (0-382-06610-3 lib. bdg.) 64 pp. Middle.

The history of castles, their role in medieval life and war, how they were built, and their decline are discussed here. The text is accompanied by color photos and illustrations.

081. Cole, Joanna. *Ms. Frizzle's Adventures: Medieval Castle*. Illus. Bruce Degen. New York: Scholastic, 2003. 44 pp. (0-590-10820-4 hc.) Elementary.

The energetic Ms. Frizzle, her student Arnold, and two others time-travel to a medieval castle that's under siege. While they save the castle from the invaders, readers learn all about medieval life and warfare from the brightly colored illustrations, the insets, and the humorous speech bubbles. The book ends with a page explaining which elements of the story are true and which are pretend, for example, that the modern and medieval characters would not really have been able to understand each other's languages so easily.

082. Delafosse, Claude. *Castles*. Illus. C. & D. Millet. 1990. Trans. Jennifer Riggs. First Discovery Books Series. New York: Scholastic, 1993. 36 pp. (0-590-46377-2 hc.) Pre-Kindergarten.

For the very youngest readers, this small, spiral-bound volume introduces the idea of life inside a castle, as well as knights, armor, and warfare. See-through plastic pages add an element of surprise; when the page is turned, you can see another part of castle life in the paintings.

083. Gravett, Christopher. *Castle*. Photos by Geoff Dann. Dorling Kindersley Eyewitness Books. New York: Alfred A. Knopf, 1994. 64 pp. (0-679-86000-2 hc.) Elementary-Middle-Junior.
Like other books in the Eyewitness series, this one is divided into topics that are each covered on one double-page spread. Each topic has a paragraph of main text and a variety of illustrations with detailed captions. The book covers a variety of kinds of castles with a focus on medieval European structures from various geographical areas (and one very misplaced chapter on "Castles in Japan"). Other topics include warfare, life inside a medieval castle, and peasant life. All of this information is about the late medieval period in Europe, making this book a solid introduction for all ages.

084. Macaulay, David. *Castle*. Boston: Houghton Mifflin, 1977. 74 pp. (0-395-25784-0 hc.) All ages.
Illustrated with elaborate pen sketches, the book tells the story of the construction of a castle in Wales at the end of the 13th century. Although the castle is fictional, it is based on the designs of actual Welsh castles of the same time period. The accuracy and detail of the pictures make this book appropriate for a person of any age who seeks information about castles and their construction. A 57-minute animated video recording based on the book is also available, directed by Jack Stokes, produced by Unicorn Projects, and distributed by Dorset Video, 1983. It uses both animation and live-action sequences, the latter featuring a discussion by David Macaulay and Sarah Bullen.

085. Macdonald, Fiona. *A Medieval Castle*. Illus. Mark Bergin. Inside Story Series. New York: Peter Bedrick Books, 1990. 48 pp. (0-87226-340-1 hc.) Elementary.
The construction of castles, including a day in a workman's life, the lives of a castle's inhabitants, its neighborhood, and its defense, are treated in one central paragraph and several colored drawings per page.

Each drawing has its own paragraph-length caption explaining another aspect of castle, village, or town life. Glossary, index.

086. Maynard, Christopher. *Days of the Knights: A Tale of Castles and Battles*. DK Readers Series (Level 4: Proficient Readers). New York: DK Publishing, 1998. 48 pp. (0-789-42963-2 pb.) Elementary.

Color photos and informational sidebars are added to the story of a fictional castle under siege. Glossary.

087. Monks, John. *The Great Book of Castles*. Vero Beach, FL: Rourke Enterprises, 1989. 48 pp. (0-86592-456-2.) Elementary.

Although information about life inside late medieval castles, warfare, and the history of European castles is included, it's the color photos and paintings of castles that make this book appealing. A few modern castles are also pictured, including Disney World's Cinderella's Castle. Glossary, index.

088. Nardo, Don. *The Medieval Castle*. Building History Series. San Diego: Lucent Books, 1998. 96 pp. (1-56006-430-7 lib. bdg.) Junior-Senior.

From their sources in classical structures to the influence of the feudal system on castle building, this book tells just as much about life inside a castle as it does about the actual construction of castles. Budding architects will find a few diagrams of parts of castles, but a greater proportion of the information is given in quotations from primary and secondary textual sources. Specific castles are often used as examples to show design problems and advances. Many of the black and white illustrations are from 19th-century sources. Glossary, further reading, bibliography, index.

089. Pipe, Jim. *Mystery History of a Medieval Castle*. Mystery History Series. Illus. Dave Burroughs et al. Brookfield, CT: Copper Beech Books, 1996. 31 pp. (0-761-30501-7 hc.) Elementary.

In double-page spreads readers see detailed watercolors of castle life and read short paragraphs of description. They are also given questions and games based on the pictures—as well as a mystery to solve: which one of the characters who appear in the pictures has tried to kill the queen? A board game is included in the back of the book.

090. Sancha, Sheila. *The Castle Story*. New York: Crowell, 1979. 224 pp. (0-690-04146-2 hc.) Junior-Senior.

In her text and her meticulously captioned drawings and photographs Sancha tells all about English castles and the people who lived in them. The history of castle building, and the history of particular castles themselves; warfare and the defense of castles; life inside and outside the castles, from the servants to the lords—all are described here. Sancha playfully superimposes drawings of medieval people and structures onto her photos of castle ruins, making this an essential book for anyone who plans to explore English castles. A map of existing castles, an illustrated glossary and chronological table, and an index supplement the text.

091. Shuter, Jane. *Carisbrooke Castle*. Visiting the Past Series. Chicago: Heinemann Library, 2000. 32 pp. (1-575-72857-5 lib. bdg.) Elementary-Middle.

Photos of the present-day castle on the Isle of Wight are interspersed with maps and drawings. In double-page spreads we learn the castle's history from Saxon times forward, its construction and ownership, and its defense (including weapons). The focus is on warfare, not daily life. Lots of technical terms are included. Time line, glossary, further reading, index.

092. Smith, Beth. *Castles*. Illus. Anne Canevari Green. New York: Franklin Watts, 1988. 96 pp. (0-531-10511-3 lib. bdg.) Middle.

Different types of castles, their history, their construction, and life inside them are discussed in detail and illustrated with black and white photos of surviving castles as well as drawings and diagrams. Readers who want to understand the difference between motte and bailey structures and concentric structures, or who want details about a portcullis or how to attack a castle, will find their answers here, along with a few of the ghost stories associated with castles in the British Isles. Glossary, further reading, index.

093. Steele, Philip. *Castles*. New York: Kingfisher, 1995. 64 pp. (1-85697-547-9 hc.) Elementary-Middle.

Short paragraphs of text and large paintings on double-page spreads tell about the construction of and life in high and late medieval castles. Armor, fashion, bathing, heraldry, food, and market day are some of the topics covered. A fold-out spread in the middle illustrates the inside and outside of a castle in a cutaway view. Time line, glossary, index.

094. Unstead, R. J. *Living in a Castle*. Illus. Victor Ambrus. Reading, MA: Addison-Wesley, 1971. 44 pp. (0-201-08495-3 hc.) Elementary.
Unstead takes readers through an imaginary English castle in the year 1250, looking into each room and noting what different people did, what they ate and wore, how they spent a typical day. His short text, and Ambrus's color and black and white drawings, is packed with details that demonstrate a thorough knowledge of the subject. In readable, economical prose, Unstead reveals a wealth of fascinating information about medieval life. Index.

095. ———. *See Inside a Castle*. 1977. New York: Warwick Press, 1986. 32 pp. (0-531-19011-0 hc.) Elementary.
Paintings illustrate the short text about the construction of, defense of, and life within a late medieval castle. The book ends with black and white photos of some famous castles. Time line, glossary, index.

096. Vaughan, Jenny. *Castles*. An Easy-Read Fact Book. New York: Franklin Watts, 1984. 32 pp. (0-531-04706-7 hc.) Elementary.
Paintings and color photos of surviving castles accompany this introduction to different types of structures, their defense, and life inside them. Each subject gets two or three paragraphs and illustrations. Glossary, index.

Art and Architecture

097. Caselli, Giovanni. *Cathedral Builder*. Photos by John James. Everyday Life Series. New York: Peter Bedrick, 1992. 32 pp. (0-872-26115-8 lib. bdg.) Elementary-Middle.
As Etienne, an apprentice to an architect, helps to build the cathedral at Rheims, he (and readers) learns about quarrying and carving stone, construction techniques, and stained glass. Further reading.

098. Corrain, Lucia. *Giotto and Medieval Art: The Lives and Works of the Medieval Artists*. Illus. Sergio and Andrea Ricciardi. New York: Peter Bedrick, 1995. Translated by Simon Knight from *Giotto e l'arte ne Medioevo*. 64 pp. (0-87226-315-0 hc.) Middle-Adult.
This large-format book is laid out in double-page spreads, each one a chapter "devoted to an aspect of the life and art of Giotto or the major

artistic and cultural developments of his time." This is one of the best books about medieval Italian art available, and its scope is much wider than just Giotto; his teacher Cimabue gets a chapter, and later, works by Cimabue and Giotto are placed side-by-side with detailed comparisons. Readers learn how artists worked and lived, the role of the church as a patron of art, what came before Giotto and why he was original, and what life was like in 13th- and 14th-century Italy. This may look like a book for younger readers, but high school students—and adults—interested in art history would do themselves a service to study it closely. It includes a section on "Where to See Works by Giotto," including several museums in the U.S. Time line, index.

099. Cox, Reg, and Neil Morris. *The Seven Wonders of the Medieval World*. Illus. James Field. Philadelphia: Chelsea House, 1995. 32 pp. (0-7910-6047-0 hc.) Elementary.

They were constructed somewhere in the world between 500–1500: that's what unifies the seven wonders in this book—the Cave of Ten Thousand Buddhas in China; the stone ruins known as Great Zimbabwe; Angkor Wat in Cambodia; the Crusader castle, Krak des Chevaliers in Syria; Salisbury Cathedral in England; the Alhambra in Spain; and Tenochtitlán, the Aztec city that lies under present-day Mexico City. Each gets a few paragraphs, a painting, and a page of photos and paintings of artifacts. Glossary, index.

100. Drogin, Marc. *Yours Truly, King Arthur: How Medieval People Wrote, and How You Can, Too*. New York: Taplinger, 1982. 95 pp. (0-800-88765-4 pb.) (Reprinted, slightly altered, as *Yours Truly, King Arthur: Calligraphy of the Middle Ages and How to Do It*. Mineola, NY: Dover, 1998. 91 pp. (0-486-40205-3 pb.) Elementary-Middle-Junior.

Drogin is a calligrapher who has written books for adults about both the history and technique of medieval calligraphy. This is an excellent introduction to calligraphy for younger readers who would like to try their own hand at it.

101. Hunt, Jonathan, writer/illus. *Illuminations*. New York: Aladdin, 1993. 40 pp. (0-689-71700-8 pb.) All ages.

This beautiful alphabet book using items from medieval life and legend as the subjects—Excalibur, Unicorn, Knight, Villein, etc.—looks like it's for younger readers, but the details and the pen and watercolor illustrations will appeal to all ages of readers. Elementary through high school teachers have successfully used it to introduce the Middle Ages to their students. Each alphabet word is explained in a few sentences; those sentences often introduce other medieval terms and ideas. Author's note, further reading, bibliography.

102. Macaulay, David. *Cathedral*. Boston: Houghton Mifflin, 1973. 80 pp. (0-395-17513-5 hc.) All ages.

The Gothic cathedral Macaulay describes here is imaginary, but the methods of construction are ones that would be used in 13th-century France. A simple text and many pen and ink illustrations make the book accessible to elementary audiences, but the wealth of architectural details invites high school and adult readers, as well. Glossary. A 60-minute video recording based on the book is also available, produced by Unicorn Projects and distributed by Dorset Video (1985). Animated sequences are narrated by Derek Jacobi, and live-action parts are hosted by David Macaulay and Caroline Berg.

103. Macdonald, Fiona. *A Medieval Cathedral*. Illus. John James. New York: Peter Bedrick Books, 1991. 48 pp. (0-872-26350-9 hc.) Elementary-Middle.

Macdonald focuses not on the building of a cathedral but on those whose lives were affected by cathedrals, from the workers in the stone quarries who didn't expect to live very long, to the pilgrims who traveled to them, to the clergy members who passed their lives within the cathedral grounds. She connects medieval cathedrals with modern ones. A double-page spread is used for each topic, and the color illustrations include some cutaway pictures.

104. Watson, Percy. *Building the Medieval Cathedrals*. Cambridge Topic Book. Cambridge: Cambridge University Press, 1976. 48 pp. (0-521-08711-2 pb.) Junior-Senior.

Readers learn in great detail how, where, and why Norman and Gothic cathedrals were built in England. Black and white illustrations show cathedral plans, tools, and construction methods, medieval representations of cathedral builders, modern photos of cathedrals, and photos of modern craftsmen at work.

105. Wilson, Elizabeth B. *Bibles and Bestiaries: A Guide to Illuminated Manuscripts.* New York: Pierpont Morgan Library and Farrar, Straus & Giroux, 1994. 64 pp. (0-347-30685-0 hc.) Junior-Senior.

Beautifully illustrated with reproductions of medieval manuscripts from the Pierpont Morgan Library and other collections, each with a lively caption, Wilson's expert work explains the history, the making, the varieties, and the uses of medieval books. She shows the role of Christianity in the spread of manuscripts, but she also includes "Other 'People of the Book.'" Older readers interested in calligraphy or the medieval period will appreciate this fine book, while younger readers will be drawn to the fascinating illustrations. Glossary.

Christianity and Monasticism

106. Boyd, Anne. *Life in a Medieval Monastery: Durham Priory in the Fifteenth Century.* (First published as *The Monks of Durham* in 1975.) Cambridge Introduction to World History. Cambridge: Cambridge University Press, 1987. 48 pp. (0-521-33724-0 pb.) Junior-Senior.

Black and white photos, maps, and drawings enhance this short but impressively informative book in which fascinating details about daily life are placed alongside information about medieval monasteries: where the money came from, how priors were elected, how new houses were founded, what monastic schools were like. Boyd focuses on the monastery at Durham and she tells the life of the seventh-century St. Cuthbert, who is buried there.

107. Caselli, Giovanni. *The Everyday Life of a Medieval Monk.* New York: Peter Bedrick, 1986. 30 pp. (0-87226-105-0 hc.) Elementary.

Set in France in 1140, this story of a noble boy who is given to the monastery at Cluny as a novice uses illustrated double-page spreads with several paragraphs of text on each to tell about topics like daily life, pilgrims, chapter houses, and final vows.

108. Harnett, Cynthia. *Monasteries and Monks.* Illus. Edward Osmond. London: B.T. Batsford, 1963. 176 pp. Junior-Senior.

Written for a British audience, and with the assumption that its readers will be familiar with some of the names and places discussed, this book, illustrated with black and white drawings, tells stories associated

with specific English monasteries. People who plan to visit some of the
establishments—including Canterbury, Westminster Abbey, Glastonbury, and St. Albans, as well as lesser-known sites—will enjoy reading
these tales about the founding and medieval histories of these places.
Maps, index.

109. McAleavy, Tony. *Life in a Medieval Abbey*. English Heritage Series.
New York: Enchanted Lion Books, 2003. 64 pp. (1-592-70006-3 hc.)
Middle-Junior.

Divided into four sections covering daily life, the origins of monastic life,
monasteries in the medieval world, and the decline of monasteries, this
book focuses on England. Readers learn about the varieties of people who
joined monasteries, the Benedictine Rule, the cultural, artistic, and scholarly contributions of medieval monks and nuns, and finally the dissolution
of the English monasteries in the 16th century under King Henry VIII.
McAleavy has written *Life in a Medieval Castle* for the same series.

110. Nardo, Don. *Life on a Medieval Pilgrimage*. The Way People Live
Series. San Diego: Lucent Books, 1995. 95 pp. (1-560-06325-4 lib.
bdg.) Junior-Senior.

Nardo begins with an overview of the supreme importance of Christianity in Western Europe from the 5th through the 15th centuries.
Once he turns to pilgrimages themselves, Nardo zeroes in on the later
Middle Ages. He uses Chaucer's Canterbury pilgrims and the 15th-
century English pilgrim Margery Kempe as illustrations, and although
he sometimes misreads medieval texts or overgeneralizes from a single
example, much of his information is helpful and lively. Readers learn
the wheres, hows, and whys of medieval pilgrimage: where people went,
how they dealt with dangers en route, and why they kept making pilgrimages in the face of such difficulties. In the last chapter Nardo
briefly discusses modern religious pilgrimages. Black and white illustrations, index, further reading, source notes.

111. Sherrow, Victoria. *Life in a Medieval Monastery*. The Way People
Live Series. San Diego: Lucent Books, 2001. 96 pp. (1-560-06791-8
hc.) Middle-Junior.

Sherrow explains how monasticism got its start in the third century before
telling about the lives of monks: who they were, what they wore, what

they ate. Sidebars give quotations from both primary and secondary sources along with little-known facts. The focus is on monks, not nuns.

Plague

112. Biel, Timothy L. *The Black Death*. World Disasters Series. San Diego: Lucent Books, 1989. 64 pp. (1-560-06001-8 hc.) Middle-Junior-Senior.
Biel looks at the causes and effects of the disease, as well as the economic and social conditions in 14th-century Europe that encouraged its spread.

113. Cohen, Daniel. *The Black Death, 1347–1351*. New York: Franklin Watts, 1974. 80 pp. (0-531-02171-8 lib. bdg.) Middle-Junior.
This overview of the Black Death is illustrated with images from medieval art.

114. Corzine, Phyllis. *The Black Death*. World History Series. San Diego: Lucent Books, 1997. 112 pp. (1-56006-299-1 lib. bdg.) Middle-Junior-Senior.
Corzine keeps her eye on 14th-century Europe as she sets the scene for the plague by introducing readers to social conditions, as well as rural and urban life. Quotations from primary and secondary sources and black and white illustrations accompany her explanation of the course of the disease, its treatment, and its social and economic effects on Europe. Time line, further reading, bibliography, index.

115. Dunn, John M. *Life During the Black Death*. The Way People Live Series. San Diego: Lucent Books, 2000. 96 pp. (1-56006-542-7 hc.) Junior-Senior.
The causes and effects of the plague that struck Europe in the 14th century are dealt with here, and Dunn distinguishes between the ways different social classes, and urban and rural people, were affected by the disease, including economic changes. Illustrations from both medieval and 19th-century sources are included. Notes, chronology, further reading, bibliography, index.

116. Nardo, Don, ed. *The Black Death*. Turning Points in World History Series. San Diego: Greenhaven, 1999. 173 pp. (1-56510-995-3 lib. bdg.) Senior.

An anthology of essays and excerpts from longer works by modern scholars and writers, some of them edited for difficulty. Each essay is summarized in a paragraph. The introduction gives an overview of the plague in medieval Europe, and the extensive appendix quotes from medieval documents about the plague. This is a useful volume for high school and college students researching the disease. Chronology, further reading, index.

117. Oleksy, Walter. *The Black Plague*. New York: Franklin Watts, 1982. 88 pp. (0-531-04426-2 lib. bdg.) Middle-Junior.

Not for the squeamish, with its black and white photos and drawings of rats, fleas, and corpses, this book traces the history, causes, and treatment of bubonic plague. Although it begins with a 1981 case of the disease and then jumps to the ancient world, most of the book deals with plague in the Middle Ages. Oleksy peppers his prose with many quotations from medieval sources, including Boccaccio's famous description of the plague in Florence, as well as lesser-known works. Further reading, index.

CHAPTER TWO

Reference Works

Some of the encyclopedic works included in this section were written specifically for young readers. Others, prepared for more general audiences, are easily accessible by teenagers. However, I have not included encyclopedias whose primary audience is scholars, and whose writers assume a great deal of knowledge from their readers.

118. Bunson, Matthew E. *Encyclopedia of the Middle Ages*. New York: Facts on File, 1995. 512 pp. (0-8160-2456-1 hc.) Junior-Senior.
This one-volume work for general readers is accessible to high school students. In addition to one- or two-paragraph entries with cross-references, black and white illustrations, and maps, the work includes an eight-page chronology from the years 410–1492.

119. Cantor, Norman, gen. ed. *The Encyclopedia of the Middle Ages*. New York: Viking, 1999. 464 pp. (0-670-10011-0 hc.) Senior.
Written for a general audience, this attractively produced, one-volume work will prove helpful to high school students. Unsigned entries range from a paragraph to a page and a half and are illustrated with both black and white and color reproductions of lesser-known works of medieval art, maps, and modern drawings. Over 600 entries cover Western Europe, Africa, and Asia, and define people, institutions, literary

and artistic works, religious movements, commerce, and facets of daily life. Cross-references, index.

120. Figg, Kristin Mossler, and John Block Friedman, eds. *Arts and Humanities through the Eras (814–1450)*. Farmington Hills, MI: Gale, forthcoming. Junior-Senior.

The nine chapters in this volume cover art, literature, music, architecture, dance, fashion, religion, philosophy, and the theater in medieval Europe. Each chapter begins with an overview of the topic before focusing on 12–24 related items; these are followed in each chapter by a chronology, definitions of key terms, biographies, excerpts from primary documents, black and white illustrations, and information about websites and audiovisual material. The editors are medievalists; their aim is to relate areas of the humanities to broad cultural trends.

121. Franck, Irene, and David Brownstone. *Dress through the Ages*. 16 vols. Danbury, CT: Grolier Educational, 2001. (0-717-29558-3 hc.) Elementary-Middle.

Each 32-page volume in this series is illustrated with photos and drawings and focuses on a particular occupation (such as surgeon, clown, ballerina, and Egyptian princess). The two volumes of interest for the Middle Ages are those on knights and pilgrims. Further reading, glossary, index.

122. Haywood, John. *World Atlas of the Past*. 4 vols. Oxford: Oxford University Press, 1999. 256 pp. (0-195-21443-9 hc.) Middle-Junior-Senior.

Five million years of human history are covered in these four volumes. The focus is on political and economic history, which is presented in a sophisticated narrative form; separate chapters look at specific leaders or eras. Sidebars, photos, maps, illustrations, and time lines are included in each chapter. Women, children, and everyday life play very little role in these volumes, and the language is not gender-neutral. The second volume, *Medieval World*, includes information about the Vikings and the rise of Islam.

123. Jordan, William C., ed. *The Middle Ages: An Encyclopedia for Students*. 4 vols. New York: Scribner, 1996. (0-684-19773-1 lib. bdg.) Junior-Senior.

An illustrated encyclopedia covering both East and West, Byzantium, Judaism, and Islam, in addition to Christianity. The 700 entries run from a paragraph to several pages. Black and white photos and maps are included, as are definitions of difficult words in the margins. The first three volumes each contain eight pages of color plates about one of the following topics: Daily Life, Art and Architecture, and People of the Middle Ages. Index.

124. ———. *The Middle Ages: A Watts Guide for Children.* New York: Scholastic Library, 2000. 112 pp. (0-531-16488-8 pb.) Middle.
Covering the years 500 to 1500 in alphabetical entries ranging from one to several pages, this encyclopedia gives very basic information along with color photos, reproductions of medieval art, or modern illustrations.

125. Knight, Judson. *The Middle Ages.* Ed. Judy Galens. U-X-L Middle Ages Reference Library Series. 4 vols. Detroit: U-X-L, 2001. Middle-Junior.
The first volume (in two parts) features biographies, the second is an almanac, the third reprints primary source material, and the fourth is a cumulative index. Volumes include time lines, glossaries, indexes, illustrations, further reading, and websites. They range from 170–230 pages and cover Eastern and Western Europe, Asia, and the Arab world. The seven-page biographies of 50 people—from Abelard and Averroës to William the Conqueror and Wu Ze-tian—are supplemented with inset biographies of other historical figures. Volume 2, *Almanac*, features prose explanations of different geographical and political areas, arranged chronologically. The 19 chapters include "The Fall of the Roman Empire," "The Islamic World," "The Turks," "The Jewish World," "The Thirteenth Century," "India," "China," "The Americas," "Africa," and "The Late Middle Ages." The 16 entries in volume 3, *Primary Sources*, are grouped into four subjects: "Cultures in Conflict" (including Anna Comnena's *Alexiad* and Usamah ibn Munquidh's *Memoirs*); "Personal Life" (including Augustine's *Confessions* and Christine de Pisan's *The Treasure of the City of Ladies*); "Church and State" (including Gregory of Tours's *History of the Franks*, Shotoku Taishi's "Seventeen-Article Constitution," and Dante's *Divine Comedy*); and "History and Fiction" (including Procopius's *Secret History* and Lo Kuan-chung's *Romance of the Three Kingdoms*). Each short

excerpt begins with an introduction and suggestions about what to consider while reading the passage. Marginal comments gloss words and inset boxes give more information.

126. *The Library of the Middle Ages.* 12 vols. New York: Rosen Publishing Group, 2003. (0-8239-7690-4 hc. Set I; 0-8239-7691-2 hc. Set II). Middle-Junior.

Each 64-page volume in this set is written by a different author and is designed to meet middle school curriculum standards. Each contains color photos, an index, and a glossary. The six volumes in Set I are: *Crusader Castles: Christian Fortresses in the Middle East; Richard the Lionheart and the Third Crusade: The English King Confronts Saladin in A.D. 1191; The First Crusade: The Capture of Jerusalem in A.D. 1099; Islamic Weapons, Warfare, and Armies: Muslim Military Operations against the Crusaders; Jerusalem under Muslim Rule in the Eleventh Century: Christian Pilgrims under Islamic Government;* and *Saladin and the Kingdom of Jerusalem: The Muslims Recapture the Holy Land in A.D. 1187.* The volumes in Set II are entitled: *Castles and Cathedrals: The Great Buildings of Medieval Times; Medieval Clothing and Costumes: Displaying Wealth and Class in Medieval Times; Damsels Not in Distress: The True Story of Women in Medieval Times; Medieval Feasts and Banquets: Food, Drink, and Celebration in the Middle Ages; Tournaments and Jousts: Training for War in Medieval Times;* and *Weapons and Warfare: Armies and Combat in Medieval Times.*

127. Loyn, H. R., ed. *The Middle Ages: A Concise Encyclopædia.* New York and London: Thames and Hudson, 1989. 352 pp. (0-500-25103-7 hc.) Senior.

A British work aimed at a general audience, this one-volume encyclopedia contains signed articles written by scholars. Articles vary in length from a short paragraph to several pages and most include a bibliography, although their references are often scholarly in nature (and not always in English). Black and white photos of medieval art and artifacts are included.

128. *Medieval World.* 10 vols. Danbury, CT: Grolier Educational, 2001. 800 pp. (0-7172-5520-4 hc.) Middle-Junior.

With 226 alphabetical entries ranging from one to seven pages and color illustrations on every page—as well as bulleted information, sidebars, maps, and time lines—this is an attractive work. Entries cover important people, places, ideas, and events, such as Peter Abelard, Jews and Judaism, Papacy, House and Home, and Education. Although the focus is on Western Europe, connections are made with Byzantium, Africa, and Asia, and the development and influence of Islam are covered. Each volume includes an index to the entire set, a glossary, a time line, and further resources (including online resources).

129. Strayer, Joseph Reese. *The Dictionary of the Middle Ages*. 13 vols. New York: Scribner, 1982. Senior.

The articles in this encyclopedia are written by scholars for a general audience, so most of them are accessible to high school students. Each entry—and they run from a paragraph to several pages in length—includes an extensive bibliography and cross-references. Black and white illustrations are also included. The last volume is an index.

CHAPTER THREE

Continental Europe, 500–1100

Judging from the number of American books published about Europe in the 6th through the 11th centuries, there is far less interest in other parts of Europe than there is in Scandinavia. You can see this particularly well by the number of titles about the Vikings. Charlemagne, the Frankish leader who was crowned Holy Roman Emperor on Christmas Day in the year 800, receives some attention in both fiction and nonfiction, but the rest of early Continental Europe is barely dealt with in books published in the United States.

Nevertheless, there was a great deal happening in the rest of Continental Europe. In the sixth century, for example, St. Benedict founded a monastery at Monte Cassino in Italy and wrote his famous Benedictine Rule; plague ravaged Western Europe; and the Lombards conquered northern Italy. In the eighth century Charles Martel battled Arabic invaders in what is now France and Pepin the Short started the Carolingian dynasty. The ninth century brought historic events like the Strasbourg Oaths, where Louis the German and Charles the Bald pledged loyalty to each other not in Latin but in their own languages, German and French. Further south, Arabs pillaged Rome and the coast of France, and in the north, St. Cyril was inventing the Cyrillic alphabet. Meanwhile, a Carolingian noblewoman named Dhuoda wrote a book teaching her son how to conduct himself properly as a Christian and as an aristocrat. And in tenth-century Germany, Hroswitha of Gandersheim, a nun, wrote plays based on Roman models; Otto I began what is known as the Ottoman Empire; and he also defeated the Magyars, superb horsemen who were invading much of central Europe. These are only a few of the political and cultural highlights of early medieval Europe, and they say nothing of the majority of Europeans, the peasants. Yet except in some of the informational books listed in chapter 1, and with the notable exception of Scandinavia, Europe in this period has been poorly represented in books published in English.

A few legendary stories of Charlemagne, particularly from *The Song of Roland*, are included within anthologies in chapter 12, "Medieval Legend and Folklore."

Nonfiction

130. Banfield, Susan. *Charlemagne*. World Leaders Past and Present Series. New York: Chelsea House Publishers, 1986. 112 pp. (0-87754-592-8 lib. bdg.) Junior.

Illustrated with inset quotations, black and white prints, maps, and family trees, this biography personalizes the late eighth- and early ninth-century ruler of the Franks by adding details about what he might have seen or thought in different stages of his life. The political background also gets told in this readable book. Further reading, chronology, index.

131. Biel, Timothy Levi. *The Importance of Charlemagne*. The Importance of Biography Series. San Diego: Lucent Books, 1997. 127 pp. (1-560-06074-3 hc.) Junior-Senior.

Illustrated with both black and white pictures (many of them from 19th-century works) and quotations from primary sources, the book focuses on the political and military history of the Carolingians. It also includes information about Charles as a person, taken from Einhard's biography. Source notes, glossary, further reading, index, time line.

132. Macdonald, Fiona. *The World in the Time of Charlemagne AD 700–900*. The World in the Time of Series. Parsippany, NJ: Dillon Press, 1978. 48 pp. (0-382-39737-1 hc.) Elementary-Middle.

Although four pages are devoted to Charlemagne, the rest of the book tells about art, religion, and political leaders in Africa, the Americas, Australia, East Asia, Europe, the Middle East, and South Asia during the years 700–900. Illustrated with beautiful photos of artifacts, the book tries to cover so much information about so many cultures that readers may be confused into thinking that all are somehow connected with Charlemagne. For example, one picture caption begins, "Khmer farmers in Charlemagne's time grew rice." Glossary, index, time line.

133. Spyeck, Jeff. *The Holy Roman Empire and Charlemagne in World History*. In World History Series. Berkeley Heights, NJ: Enslow, 2002. 128 pp. (0-766-01901-2 lib. bdg.) Middle.

A biography of Charlemagne as a warrior, a Christian king, and an empire builder.

Fiction

134. Almedingen, E. M. *A Candle at Dusk*. Illus. Doreen Roberts. New York: Farrar, Straus & Giroux, 1969. 150 pp. Middle.

An eighth-century Frankish boy lives at an abbey because he wants to learn to read, but his community lives in the fear of a Saracen invasion. When it comes, the Saracens sack the abbey.

135. Manson, Christopher, writer/illus. *Two Travelers*. New York: Henry Holt, 1990. 32 pp. (0-8050-1214-1 hc.) Elementary.

In 787, a servant brings an elephant from Baghdad to France as a gift from the caliph to Charlemagne. The servant, Isaac, and the elephant form a bond. The story is based on a historical event.

136. Westwood, Jennifer. *Stories of Charlemagne*. 1972. New York: S. G. Phillips, 1976. 153 pp. (0-87599-213-7 hc.) Junior.

In a substantial introduction, Westwood, a scholar of the medieval period, explains how a Germanic king became a French national hero, and she provides readers with both a biography of Charlemagne and information about the Old French chansons de geste in which stories and legends of his life were told in the 12th and 13th centuries. The stories she retells are taken from chansons de geste (including *The Song of Roland*) and romances, and she puts them in chronological order of Charlemagne's life, from his origins to his old age. Author's note.

137. Willard, Barbara. *Son of Charlemagne*. Illus. Emil Weiss. 1959. Bathgate, ND: Bethlehem Books, 1998. 208 pp. (1-883-93730-2 pb.) Middle-Junior.

Set in the years 781–800, the year Charlemagne was crowned Holy Roman Emperor, and based in part on Einhard's *Life of Charlemagne*, this is the story of the Frankish king, told from the perspective of his son. The book begins with Charlemagne taking his entire family with him on a journey over the Alps to Rome. Historical figures like the English scholar Alcuin make appearances. Author's note.

CHAPTER FOUR

The Vikings

The Vikings hold a strong grip on the American imagination, as the numerous books about them suggest. Despite the popular view of Vikings as frightening warriors, most of the books demonstrate the complexity and richness of the Viking legacy. Their lives as explorers, traders, and farmers are often featured, as well as their craftsmanship with jewelry, coins, and ships. A number of books touch on the Norse explorers who landed in North America, and some books take care to include information about Iceland's Althing, considered to be the first European parliament. The relatively high status of Viking women (at least, in comparison with women in high and late medieval Europe) plays a role in both fiction and nonfiction, as does the conversion to Christianity. Books about Norse mythology can be found in chapter 12, "Medieval Legends and Folklore."

We know about the Vikings from a variety of different sources. *The Anglo-Saxon Chronicle* contains many references to them, since Vikings terrorized the Anglo-Saxons in the ninth century, and later, many Scandinavians settled in the north of England. Frankish annals, kept by French monks, report Viking raids in what is now France and Germany. In the tenth century the Muslim traveler Ibn Fadlan wrote about the Viking funeral he witnessed, and a Moorish traveler, Al-Tartushi, wrote about his visit to the port town of Hedeby. Even the Byzantine emperor Constantine VII wrote about the Vikings, whom he knew since they served as guards in Constantinople. Another European writer, Adam of Bremen, wrote about the Vikings in the 11th century, although he based his words on what other people had said. The Vikings tell their own stories in the sagas, most of which were written down in the 13th century. The Vinland and Greenland sagas tell of their explorations and settlements, and archeological digs at places like L'Anse Aux Meadows in Nova Scotia have confirmed some of what the sagas record. Excavations in towns like Hedeby and York have revealed a great deal about the daily life of Viking town dwellers and have kept readers interested in the Norse people.

Nonfiction

138. Atkinson, Ian. *Viking Ships*. A Cambridge Topic Book. Minneapolis: Lerner Publications, 1980. 52 pp. (0-8225-1221-1 pb.) Junior-Senior.
If you want to know how Viking ships were built, how they worked, what varieties of ships there were, and where they have been found, this is an excellent source. Drawings, photos, and maps are included, as is an account of the 1893 building and voyage of *Viking*, a replica of the Gokstad ship. Index.

139. Buehr, Walter, writer/illus. *The Viking Explorers*. New York: Putnam's, 1967. 92 pp. Middle-Junior.
Illustrated with two-color sketches, this book begins with a Viking raid on a Frankish village before reminding readers that not all Vikings were warriors. Although Buehr includes information about Vikings as explorers and farmers, his focus is on ships—about which he tells a great deal—and fighting, including the ninth-century attack on Paris. Women play little role in this book. Index.

140. Carter, Avis Murton. *One Day with the Vikings*. New York: Abelard-Schuman, 1974. 48 pp. (0-200-00137-X hc.) Elementary-Middle.
Set in a Viking village in 850, the book takes us through a day in the lives of several people—the chieftain and his wife, a blacksmith, a warrior, and a poet, as well as their children. The substantial, informative

text is illustrated with black and white and color photos, drawings, and reproductions of medieval art.

141. Caselli, Giovanni. *A Viking Settler*. Everyday Life Series. 1986. New York: Peter Bedrick Books, 1992. 30 pp. (0-872-26104-2 lib. bdg.) Elementary.

Using double-page spreads as chapters, this book tells about the Vikings through the story of Egil, a boy living in tenth-century Hedeby, one of the famous Viking towns. Readers get glimpses of Egil's merchant father's adventures, life in town and on a farm, blood feuds and ship burials, and Viking government and literature. In the end, Egil's family moves to England. Picture glossary, further reading.

142. Clare, John D., ed. *The Vikings*. Living History Series. 1991. New York: Gulliver Books / Harcourt Brace Jovanovich, 1992. 64 pp. (0-152-00512-9 hc.) Middle-Junior.

Staged photographs with live models (both adults and children) make this a fascinating and appealing book. Each double-page spread contains a photo with inset text about topics like shipbuilding, slaves, the Vikings in Vinland (modern-day Newfoundland), runes, government, and the Danegeld. In the sections about the conversion of the Vikings to Christianity, the relationship between religion and power is emphasized. Norse words are sprinkled throughout the text (the editors engaged scholars as advisers). The final section explains the sources historians and archeologists use to know about the Vikings—and some of the problems with those sources. Time line, index.

143. D'Aulaire, Ingri, and Edgar Parin D' Aulaire. *Leif the Lucky*. Garden City, NY: Doubleday and Company, 1941. 62 pp. Elementary.

Using their distinctive style of drawing soft pencil figures on stone, as well as decorative interlace patterns from Scandinavian art, the D'Aulaires tell the story of Leif from boyhood to manhood and his journey to North America. The book is dated by its portrayal of Native Americans and "squat-legged Eskimos waddling in the ice and snow," but its illustrations still have the power to charm.

144. Finney, Fred. *Mystery History of a Viking Longboat*. Illus. Mike Bell et al. Mystery History Series. Brookfield, CT: Copper Beech Books, 1997. 32 pp. (0-761-30590-4 hc.) Middle.

Combining fiction and fact (and not always clarifying which is which), the book offers games, puzzles, and an ongoing mystery as a way to entice readers into learning about Viking explorers and their ships.

145. Gibb, Christopher. *A Viking Sailor*. Illus. John James. How They Lived Series. Vero Beach, FL: Roarke Enterprises, 1987. 32 pp. (0-86592-141-5 hc.) Elementary.
First published in England and illustrated with paintings and color photos of artifacts, this text emphasizes the many aspects of Viking life: their shipbuilding, sailing, and navigation skills, their exploring and trading—and their reputation as fearsome warriors. Home life and religion are also mentioned. Glossary, index.

146. Grant, Neil. *Eric the Red: The Viking Adventurer*. Illus. Victor Ambrus. What's Their Story? Series. New York: Oxford University Press, 1998. 32 pp. (0-19-521431-5 hc.) Elementary.
Accompanied by full-color illustrations, this excellent biography of Leif Eriksson's father briefly tells about his childhood but focuses on his adult life; after being outlawed, he discovered and settled in Greenland. When the other Greenlanders converted to Christianity, Erik held on to the old ways. Meanwhile, his son Leif sailed for North America. Author's note, index.

147. ———. *The Vikings*. Spotlights Series. New York: Oxford University Press, 1998. 46 pp. (0-195-21393-9 hc.) Elementary-Middle.
Illustrated double-page spreads feature a one-paragraph introduction, a color painting, and inset art and sentences on topics like slaves, ships, and townspeople. "Spotlights" run along the bottom of each page—four or five illustrations with accompanying short text related to the main topic. The page about "Towns" includes the spotlights "Comb," "Cloak Pin," "Well," "Rushes," and "Honey." This is a good introduction to the Vikings. Glossary, index.

148. Heath, Ian. *The Vikings*. Illus. Angus McBride. Oxford: Osprey Publishing, 1985. 64 pp. (0-850-45565-0 pb.) Middle-Junior-Senior.
Color plates illustrate this military history of the Vikings, published by a company known for its authoritative military histories.

149. Hook, Jason. *The Vikings*. New York: Thomson Learning, 1993. 32 pp. Elementary-Middle.

Each eye-catching double-page spread includes a short paragraph about a topic ("The Viking Language," "Daily Life," "Religion," "War"), supplemented by longer paragraphs keyed to color photos of three or four Viking artifacts. Glossary, index, time line, further reading.

150. Hughes, Jill. *Vikings*. Illus. Ivan Lapper; consultant, John Reeve. Find Out About Series. New York: Franklin Watts, 1984. 32 pp. (0-531-03481-X lib. bdg.) Elementary-Middle.

This simply written text focuses on the Vikings as pirates, raiders, and shipbuilders. Women's and children's roles are not discussed. The color paintings on the double-page spreads lack distinction. Glossary, index.

151. Humble, Richard. *The Age of Leif Eriksson*. Illus. Richard Hook. Exploration through the Ages Series. New York: Franklin Watts, 1989. 32 pp. (0-531-10741-8 lib. bdg.) Elementary.

Focusing on Vikings as explorers and settlers instead of warriors, Humble explains the expeditions to Iceland, to Greenland, and to North America. Color paintings, maps, glossary, time line, index.

152. Irwin, Constance. *Strange Footprints on the Land: Vikings in America*. New York: Harper and Row, 1980. 182 pp. (0-06-022773-7 lib. bdg.) Junior-Senior.

Using evidence from the sagas, Irwin recounts Bjarni Herjolfsson's tenth-century voyage to North America, along with journeys made by other Viking explorers and settlers. She explores the reasons Americans know so little about these people, and then examines the controversies and evidence about the Norse settlements in North America. Further reading, index.

153. James, John, and Louise James. *How We Know about the Vikings*. How We Know About Series. New York: Peter Bedrick Books, 1997. 32 pp. (0-872-26535-8 hc.) Elementary-Middle.

The double-page spreads introduce readers both to Viking life (with an emphasis on everyday life, not raiding war parties) and to archeology. Paintings of Viking life are shadowed by paintings of the archeological digs used to reconstruct the scene, as well as pictures of the recovered artifacts. This interesting book shows how historical evidence must be interpreted. Glossary, index, time line.

154. Jensen, Malcolm C. *Leif Erikson the Lucky*. Visual Biography Series. New York: Franklin Watts, 1979. 58 pp. (0-531-02297-8 lib. bdg.) Elementary-Middle.

The violent childhood of Leif's father Erik is presented with comparisons between the way laws work now and the way they worked in tenth-century Iceland. Erik's voyage to Greenland and the settlement there set the stage for Leif's story, and his journey to North America. Although the title page says, "Illustrated with authentic prints and documents," and although a caption to a photo tells us that winged helmets were the invention of "19th-century romantic writers," pictures of Vikings in winged helmets recur frequently throughout the book. Many of the black and white photos of artifacts are murky. Index.

155. Kimmel, Elizabeth Cody. *Before Columbus: The Leif Eriksson Expedition*. Landmark Books Series. New York: Random House, 2003. 128 pp. (0-375-81347-0 hc.) Elementary-Middle.

The stories of both Erik the Red and his son Leif are told here and readers learn about their pillaging and their exploring. We hear Leif thinking about his actions in this book, which makes it read more like a novel than straight history, but Kimmel discusses what she has added to the historical record. The illustrations include maps of artifacts taken from archeological sites. Further reading, index.

156. Macdonald, Fiona. *A Viking Town*. Illus. Mark Bergin. Inside Story Series. New York: Peter Bedrick Books, 1995. 48 pp. (0-872-26382-7 lib. bdg.) Elementary-Middle.

Focusing on the Vikings who stayed home, Macdonald's book is divided into illustrated, double-page spreads, each about a topic such as "A Viking Home," "Sports and Pastimes," and "The Shipyard." Two to three paragraphs of informative text on each spread are supplemented by annotated and labeled color paintings. Filled with fascinating details like a list of tools in a Viking kitchen, the book is a good overview. Time line, glossary, index.

157. ———— *Vikings*. Insights Series. Hauppauge, NY: Barron's Educational, 1992. 57 pp. (0-8120-6375-9 lib. bdg.) Elementary.

In this impressive, large-format book filled with color photos, maps, and drawings, readers learn about archeological and textual evidence for the Vikings in addition to Viking life. Subjects include rural and urban life, fishing, raiding, trading, the arts, Norse religion, and the conversion to Christianity. Photos of modern turf houses and features of the Icelandic landscape appear in addition to the usual swords, brooches, and rune-stones. Some pages unfold to reveal hidden scenes. Time line, glossary, index.

158. Margeson, Susan M. *Viking*. Photos by Peter Anderson. DK Eyewitness Books. New York: Knopf, 1994. 64 pp. (0-679-86002-9 hc.) Elementary-Middle.

DK's Eyewitness series combines fascinating color photos of artifacts, artwork, and reenactments with snippets of reliable text. This volume shows Vikings as sailors, warriors, traders, explorers, and farmers. Index.

159. Martell, Hazel Mary. *Food and Feasts with the Vikings*. Parsippany, NJ: New Discovery Books, 1995. 32 pp. (0-02-726317-7 lib. bdg.) Elementary.

The book begins with an introduction to the Vikings as fierce raiders, then looks at farm life, town life, and the traveling life—and the different ways urban and rural people, as well as travelers, got food. Much of the book, including the color photos, is about the lives of the Vikings, not specifically about their eating habits. Although no Viking recipes survive, the book ends with recipes for food "very much like" what the Vikings might have eaten: porridge, parsley butter, broiled salmon, pork and leek stew, and baked trout. Glossary, further reading, index.

160. ———. *Over 900 Years Ago: With the Vikings*. Illus. Roger Payne. History Detectives Series. New York: Silver Burdett, 1993. 32 pp. (0-027-26325-8 lib. bdg.) Middle.

Using artifacts from archeological digs, Martell explains what we know about the way the Vikings lived.

161. ———. *The Vikings*. Worlds of the Past Series. New York: New Discovery Books, 1992. 64 pp. Elementary.

Small photos, paintings, and maps decorate each double-page spread. The accompanying text briefly discusses archeological and written evidence about past lives before moving on to those lives themselves: food, clothing, families, and laws, as well as trading, raiding, and settling. Several matters of speculation are presented as fact. Glossary, time line, index.

162. ———. *The Vikings and Jorvik*. Hidden Worlds Series. New York: Dillon Press, 1993. 32 pp. (0-875-18541-X lib. bdg.) Elementary.
Double-page spreads illustrated with photos and paintings use the town of Jorvik (modern York, England) to illuminate everyday Viking life. The book also explores why and how archeologists learned about Jorvik (radiocarbon dating, dendochronology, environmental archeology). Photos of artifacts are supplemented by paintings of what Jorvik may have looked like. Vikings as warriors are deemphasized. Instead they are presented as traders, merchants, and craftspeople. Yet there's little here about daily family life. Glossary, index.

163. Millard, Anne. *Eric the Red: The Vikings Sail the Atlantic*. Austin, TX: Raintree Steck-Vaughn, 1994. 46 pp. (0-8114-7252-3 hc.) Elementary-Middle.
Appealing color photos, drawings, and maps accompany an impressive text, which explains the ways we study Vikings (through archeology as well as literature), tells about their lives (both the farmers and the sailors), and sets them within their chronological and geological contexts. The book also discusses Viking explorations and settlements in Greenland and North America, but the focus is not, as the title suggests, on Erik the Red. This is a good introduction to Vikings in general. Glossary, bibliography, index.

164. Morley, Jacqueline. *First Facts about the Vikings*. Illus. Mark Bergin. Created and designed by David Salariya. First Facts About Series. New York: Peter Bedrick Books, 1996. 31 pp. (0-872-26497-1 hc.) Elementary.
After an introduction raises the picture of Vikings as savage warriors, the rest of the book presents double-page spreads containing "FACTS" designed to set the record straight, showing Vikings as "law-abiding citizens," as farmers, as skillful craftspeople, even as Christian saints. However, a strong emphasis on "fact" overshadows the importance of historical interpretation—even Viking thoughts and emotions are treated as matters of fact. Glossary, index.

165. Mulvihill, Margaret. *Viking Longboats.* History Highlights Series. New York: Gloucester Press, 1989. 32 pp. (0-531-17168-X hc.) Elementary.

Although the title suggests this book will focus on ships and shipbuilding, readers also learn about the daily life and travels of the Vikings.

166. Place, Robin. *The Vikings.* New York: Warwick Press, 1980. 44 pp. (0-531-09170-8 hc.) Elementary-Middle.

This overview of Viking life and culture, including sections about poetry and sagas, Norse religion, and the coming of Christianity, is illustrated with paintings and color photos of metalwork, ships, and manuscripts. Glossary, time line, index.

167. Pluckrose, Henry, ed. *Vikings.* Illus. Ivan Lapper. Small World Series. New York: Gloucester Press, 1982. 32 pp. (0-531-03457-7 lib. bdg.) Elementary.

This brief overview of the Vikings, written for an early-elementary audience, is illustrated with paintings as well as a few photos of artifacts. Index.

168. Speed, Peter. *Life in the Time of Harald Hardrada and the Vikings.* Illus. Richard Hook. A Mirabel Book. Austin, TX: Steck-Vaughn, 1993. 63 pp. Elementary-Middle.

In chapters illustrated with paintings and photos Speed uses appealing characters and stories from Scandinavian history and mythology, and quotations from medieval texts, to introduce readers to the Vikings who raided and explored. Although farm and town life is mentioned, the focus is on politics and fighting. Glossary, index.

169. Steele, Philip. *Step into the Viking World.* Consultant: Leslie Webster, British Museum. New York: Lorenz Books, 1998. 64 pp. (1-859-67685-5 hc.) Elementary-Middle-Junior.

Double-page spreads illustrated with paintings and photos of Viking artifacts, including saga manuscripts, reveal the history and social behaviors of the Vikings. Useful and accessible activities for elementary through junior high school students—for example, making rune-stones, jewelry, and models of longships and houses, and baking bread—decorate the bottoms of several pages. This is an impressive book that uses fascinating historical information in an enticing way. Glossary, index.

170. Streissguth, Thomas. *Life among the Vikings*. The Way People Live Series. San Diego: Lucent Books, 1999. 96 pp. (1-560-06392-0 hc.) Middle-Junior-Senior.

Streissguth begins by acknowledging the distance between the imaginative view of Vikings and the reality, and the difficulty in determining that reality. The Vikings left little evidence about themselves, and all of it must be interpreted. A brief, clear history of the Viking raids and settlements in the British Isles and Europe during the ninth and tenth centuries precedes accounts of ships and fighting, social structures, and everyday life. Streissguth shows the Vikings as farmers, traders, and raiders, and he discusses their language, literature, and religion. Despite an overreliance on 19th-century visual images, this book is full of useful, clearly presented information. Source notes, time line, annotated bibliography, suggestions for further reading, index.

171. Windrow, Martin. *The Viking Warrior*. Illus. Angus McBride. The Soldier through the Ages Series. New York: Franklin Watts, 1984. 32 pp. (0-531-03816-5 hc.) Elementary.

Windrow keeps his focus on military history: the ships, weapons, and fighting tactics that made Viking men fearsome warriors. Full-page paintings accompany the three to four paragraphs of text on each double-page spread. Glossary, time line, index.

172. Wright, Rachel. *Vikings: Facts, Things to Make, Activities*. Craft Topics Series. New York: Franklin Watts, 1992. 32 pp. (0-531-14210-8 lib. bdg.) Elementary.

As she introduces readers to the Vikings as raiders, settlers, and traders, Wright includes step-by-step activities—constructing a cardboard longboat, and making clay jewelry, papier-mâché battle-axes, helmets, and shields. Color photos of each activity and paintings of Viking life illustrate the text. Glossary, further reading, index.

Fiction

173. Benchley, Nathaniel. *Beyond the Mists*. New York: Harper and Row, 1975. 152 pp. (06-020459-1 hc.) Junior.

Using the sagas as a source, Benchley constructs a novel about the Norse people in North America in the 11th century. His Danish narrator,

Gunnar Egilson, is an old man looking back on his youth. When he was 17 he killed a monk on his first raiding trip to England; on his second, when things went sour, he vowed never to kill another man. Instead he gets work on a ship, and when it wrecks, becomes a servant to King Olav Tryggvesson, who has him baptized as a Christian. Finally he joins Leif Eriksson's crew when it sails to Vinland. Gunnar often breaks into his narrative to give his readers mini history lessons.

174. ———. *Snorri and the Strangers.* Illus. Don Bolognese. An I Can Read History Book. New York: Harper and Row, 1976. 59 pp. (0-06-020458-3 lib. bdg.) Elementary.

Snorri is a little boy born in a Norse settlement in the New World; the strangers are the Native Americans the Norse people meet. This easy-to-read book includes the familiar elements of the trading of red cloth for furs, the bull that frightened the Native Americans, their subsequent hostility, and the Norse people's return to Greenland. Author's note.

175. Branford, Henrietta. *The Fated Sky.* 1996. Cambridge, MA: Candlewick Press, 1999. 156 pp. (0-7637-0775-4 hc.) Senior.

In this dark tale for older readers, Ran matures from a 16-year-old farm girl to a young wife and mother after the deaths of her family—and after she is falsely accused of murdering her own mother. Escaping from Norway to Iceland with a blind singer, Ran leaves behind her grandmother and her childhood, but danger and death are ever present. In Ran's pre-Christian world, sacrifices to the Norse deities are common, and raiders kill infants with no remorse.

176. Cadnum, Michael. *Daughter of the Wind.* New York: Orchard Books, 2003. 272 pp. (0-439-35224-X hc.) Junior-Senior.

In this stand-alone companion volume to *Raven of the Waves* 17-year-old Hallgerd is kidnapped from her Norwegian village by Danes. When she escapes, she meets Gauk, a young berserker, and Hego, who has come from home to try to rescue her. But instead of finding safety, the three encounter danger far from home.

177. ———. *Raven of the Waves.* New York: Orchard Books, 2001. 208 pp. (0-531-30334-hc.) Junior-Senior.

In 793, the lives of two boys, the 17-year-old Viking Lidsmod and the 13-year-old Anglo-Saxon Wiglaf, become intertwined when Lidsmod's ship attacks Wiglaf's village—the Vikings are looking for gold that they know is available in churches. Wiglaf, a crippled healer, is taken captive. Violence is a way of life for the Vikings, and Cadnum doesn't shirk from showing it. He skillfully weaves Norse and Anglo-Saxon words and details about Viking society and religion into the story.

178. Carter, Peter. *Madatan*. Illus. Victor Ambrus. 1974. London: Oxford University Press, 1987. 207 pp. (0-192-71359-0 hc.) Middle-Junior.
At the end of the war-torn eighth century, an Anglo-Saxon boy who has been taken by the Vikings ends up finding a life in the church in Northumbria.

179. Clements, Bruce. *Prison Window, Jerusalem Blue*. New York: Farrar, Straus & Giroux, 1977. 241 pp. (0-374-36121-5 hc.) Middle-Junior.
In the ninth century, two Anglo-Saxon children are captured by Vikings and taken to Denmark to become slaves.

180. De Angeli, Marguerite, writer/illus. *The Black Fox of Lorne*. New York: Doubleday, 1956. 191 pp. Middle.
Twin brothers sail from Norway to Scotland in the tenth century. When their father is killed and one of the boys is captured, they use their physical similarity to trick their enemies and take revenge. Newbery Honor.

181. Foster, Scarlett Ryan. *The Secret of the Viking Dagger*. San Antonio: LangMarc Publishing, 1997. 136 pp. (1-880-292-55-6 pb.) Middle.
When they come across a buried treasure chest, two boys time-travel from 20th-century Michigan to 10th-century Norway, where they meet Olaf, a Viking. His village's children have been kidnapped, and the boys help him find them, traveling through Europe and to Africa. The book often reads like a history textbook instead of a novel. Foster unconvincingly bypasses the language problems: because their grandmother speaks Norwegian, Ben and David find they can understand Old Norse; some of the Vikings also speak Anglo-Saxon, which the boys understand with no problem. Glossary, bibliography, activities.

182. French, Allen, writer/illus. *The Story of Grettir the Strong*. 1908. New York: Dutton, 1966. 268 pp. Middle-Junior.
A prose retelling of the Icelandic *Grettir's Saga*. French simplifies the chronology and streamlines the narrative to make it easier for young

readers to follow. Although Grettir lived in the 10th century, the saga was written down in the 13th century, and elements of the supernatural were incorporated into it, like trolls and giants; they also appear in French's retelling. French also adapted *Njál's Saga* in his 1905 *Heroes of Iceland*.

183. ———. *The Story of Rolf and the Viking Bow*. 1904. Bathgate, ND: Bethlehem Books, 1994. 252 pp. (1-883937-01-9 pb.) Middle-Junior.
Set in Iceland in 1010, the book draws on the Icelandic sagas for plot and style, including verses that characters sometimes converse in. Sixteen-year-old Rolf excels at archery. He and Grani are the sons of two feuding families, yet when they are threatened by a common enemy, they must fight together. Introduction, pronunciation guide, glossary.

184. Friel, Maeve. *Distant Voices*. 1994. Dublin: Poolbeg Press, 1995. 107 pp. (1-853-71410-0.) Junior.
Ellie, a contemporary Irish teenager, is haunted by the ghost of Harald, a Viking boy whose spirit she must free. Although this is a time-travel fantasy, readers learn about the Vikings in Ireland.

185. Haugaard, Erik Christian. *Hakon of Rogen's Saga*. Illus. Leo and Diane Dillon. Boston: Houghton Mifflin, 1963. 132 pp. Junior.
In Norway at the end of the Viking age, young Hakon tells of his chieftain father's second marriage and of the feud that results. When his father is killed Hakon is at risk. With the help of a Christian slave and people loyal to his father, he takes back his birthright at age 13. Responsibly written, showing both the positive and negative aspects of Viking society, the book is continued in *A Slave's Tale*.

186. ———. *A Slave's Tale*. Illus. Leo and Diane Dillon. Boston: Houghton Mifflin, 1965. 217 pp. Junior-Senior.
Picking up where *Hakon of Rogen's Saga* ended, teenage Helga tells of her newfound freedom at Hakon's hands and the journey to Frankland to return Rark, another former slave, to his home. Helga, born a slave, struggles with her self-perception and the idea of a slave mentality. The novel also portrays the coming of Christianity to Europe. Lyrical, brutal, and philosophical, the text portrays the Viking era accurately.

187. Katz, Welwyn Wilton. *Out of the Dark*. 1995. Toronto: Groundwood Books, 2001. 185 pp. (0-88899-262-9 pb.) Junior.
This is a contemporary novel with flashbacks to the eleventh-century Norse settlement in Newfoundland. Ben's recently deceased mother has told him stories of the Vikings. Visiting L'Anse aux Meadows, Ben imagines himself as a shipbuilder who journeyed to the New World and encountered the skraelings, as the Vikings called the Native Americans. Katz skillfully incorporates material from *The Vinland Sagas*, Norse texts that record that settlement, as she re-creates Viking life. Author's note.

188. Lunge-Larsen, Lise. *The Race of the Birkebeiners*. Illus. Mary Azarian. Boston: Houghton Mifflin, 2001. 32 pp. (0-618-10313-9 hc.) Elementary.
Based on a Norwegian historical episode from 1206 and illustrated with beautiful colored woodcuts, this book tells about the escape of a queen with her baby son with the help of peasants who were expert skiers. Today the event is symbolically portrayed in Birkebeiner ski races.

189. Mullen, Michael. *Sea Wolves from the North*. 1983. St. John's, Newfoundland: Breakwater Books, 1986. 96 pp. (0-920-91103-X pb.) Middle-Junior.
On the island of Iona (off the west coast of Scotland) Irish monks must protect the famous manuscript, the Book of Kells, from Viking raiders. Told from the point of view of Diarmuid, a young scribe, the book shows sympathy for both the Vikings and the monks, and it skillfully portrays the lives of both cultures.

190. Polland, Madeleine A. *Beorn the Proud*. Illus. Joan Coppa Drennen. Warsaw, ND: Bethlehem Books, 1999. 185 pp. (1-883-93709-6 pb.) Middle-Junior.
In the ninth century, Beorn is a 12-year-old Viking on his first raid. Ness is the daughter of an Irish chieftain who is captured during the raid and taken back to Denmark. Although Beorn and Ness are at odds, particularly about religion (Ness is a Christian), they slowly become friends.

191. Ritchie, Rita. *Ice Falcon*. New York: Norton, 1963. 240 pp. Junior.
Set in medieval Iceland. Bibliography.

192. Sutcliff, Rosemary. *Blood Feud.* 1976. New York: Dutton, 1977. 144 pp. (0-525-26730-1 hc.) Junior.

In the tenth century, Jestyn, a young Englishman, becomes a slave to the Viking Thormod. After he saves Thormod's life, they swear to be brothers—which involves Jestyn in Thormod's blood feud against the men who killed his father. This leads them on a journey to Constantinople, where they become members of the Varangian Guard. Later, after Thormod has died, Jestyn becomes a healer.

193. ———. *The Shield Ring.* Illus. C. Walter Hodges. 1956. New York: Walck, 1962. 215 pp. Junior-Senior.

When William the Conqueror razes England, a young Saxon woman, Frytha, escapes to the Lake District, which is inhabited by Norse settlers. She becomes friends with Bjorn, an orphan who becomes both a warrior and a minstrel. Bjorn's fear of his own cowardice, and the steps he takes to prove his courage, provide much of the tension in the book. Carnegie Commendation.

194. ———. *Sword Song.* New York: Farrar, Straus & Giroux, 1997. 272 pp. (0-374-37363-9 hc.) Junior-Senior.

Sutcliff's last novel (published posthumously and finished by others) takes place among the Vikings and the feuding Scottish clans in the early Middle Ages. Sixteen-year-old Bjarni is banished for five years from his Viking settlement in the north of England because he has killed a man in anger. He becomes a mercenary, traveling on ships to Dublin, the Scottish islands, and finally Wales, where he is shipwrecked. Angharad heals him; later, he rescues—and marries—her.

195. Treece, Henry. *The Burning of Njal.* New York: Criterion, 1964. 191 pp. Junior.

A prose retelling of *Njál's Saga.*

196. ———. *Horned Helmet.* Illus. Charles Keeping. New York: Criterion, 1963. 119 pp. Junior.

In Iceland around the year 1015, orphaned Beorn is rescued by a Viking warrior with whom he lives and travels, becoming his foster son. Treece tries to use saga style here and he weaves fragments of Anglo-Saxon poetry and incidents from sagas into his text. His firm understanding of Viking life is evident. Author's note.

197. ———. *The Last Viking*. Illus. Charles Keeping. 1964. New York: Pantheon, 1966. 146 pp. Junior.

This is the story of Harald Hardrada, who died fighting King Harold Godwinson at the Battle of Stamford Bridge in 1066. Treece begins at the battle, then flashes back to Hardrada's youthful adventures and his travels to Byzantium and Russia.

198. ———. *The Road to Miklagard*. Illus. Christine Price. New York: Criterion Books, 1957. 254 pp. Junior.

In the second volume of Harald Sigurdson's story (begun in *Viking's Dawn*), he befriends a giant, Grummoch, and travels to Constantinople with him to join the Varangian Guard.

199. ———. *Splintered Sword*. Illus. Charles Keeping. New York: Duell, Sloan and Pearce, 1965. 135 pp. Middle-Junior.

In the Orkney Islands in 1098, 15-year-old Runolf, an orphaned thrall who is mistreated by his foster family, leaves his shepherding life to become a Viking. But this life appeals to him as little as his old life and in the end, he discovers a better place, serving a Norman earl. Maps are included.

200. ———. *Swords from the North*. (Alternate title: *The Northern Brothers*.) Illus. Charles Keeping. New York: Pantheon, 1967. 240 pp. Junior.

Based on Snorri Sturluson's *Heimskringla*, or the "Sagas of the Kings" (written in the 13th century), this novel focuses on the historical figure Harald Hardrada, who was a captain of the Varangian Guard in 11th-century Byzantium.

201. ———. *Viking's Dawn*. Illus. Christine Price. New York: Criterion Books, 1956. 253 pp. Junior.

In 780, after his lord has died, 15-year-old Harald Sigurdson finds a new one in Thorkell Fairhair. Harald sails with him in his longship, harrying villagers in the Hebrides, until they are shipwrecked and captured. Harald alone makes it home. Author's note. Harald's story continues in *The Road to Miklagard* and *Viking's Sunset*.

202. ———. *Viking's Sunset*. Illus. Christine Price. New York: Criterion, 1960. 182 pp. Junior.

In the last tale of Harald Sigurdson, he is a 40-year-old farmer and the headman of his village; the year is 815. When berserkers attack the village in his absence, he leaves Norway to seek revenge. His voyage takes him to Iceland, Greenland, and, finally, North America, where he meets a variety of rather stereotyped Native Americans. In this volume Treece imitates saga style, with limited success. Author's note.

203. ———. *Westward to Vinland*. Illus. William Stobbs. New York: S. G. Phillips, 1967. 192 pp. Junior.

Drawing on the Icelandic sagas, Treece tells the stories of Erik the Red, his son Leif, and the Viking voyages to North America.

CHAPTER FIVE

British Isles, 500–1066

Ireland

Despite Ireland's popularity in America, writers for young readers have barely touched the history of early medieval Ireland. Brian Boru, the king who briefly united Ireland in the 11th century, has inspired a few works, as have some Irish saints—especially those associated with manuscripts, such as St. Columba. Much more has been written about Irish legends, and some of those works are listed in chapter 12, "Medieval Legends and Folklore." Because there are so few books about early medieval Irish history, fiction and nonfiction are grouped together in this section.

204. Andrew, J. S. *The Green Hill of Nendrum.* (Alternate title: *The Bell of Nendrum.*) 1969. New York: Hawthorn Books, 1970. Belfast: Blackstaff Press, 1985. 200 pp. (0-856-40341-5 pb.) Junior.
A 15-year-old boy from the 20th century time-travels to 10th-century Ireland and meets the monks at a monastery he knows will be destroyed by the Vikings. Although he fights with them, he is unable to save the monks, but he brings a bell and a chalice forward in time with him.

205. Brown, Don, writer/illus. *Across a Dark and Wild Sea.* Brookfield, CT: Roaring Brook Press, 2002. 32 pp. (0-7613-2415-1 lib. bdg.) Elementary.

Columcille, or St. Columba, was a sixth-century Irish monk who revered books and became a scribe. After a battle instigated by a book of psalms in which 3,000 people died, he left Ireland for the Scottish island of Iona where, along with 12 followers, he started a monastery. Gorgeous watercolors and Celtic designs illustrate this biography, which also includes information about manuscript making and an uncial alphabet. Deborah Nadel's calligraphy enhances the book's appeal. Author's note, bibliography.

206. Corfe, Tom. *St. Patrick and Irish Christianity.* Cambridge Topic Book. Cambridge: Cambridge University Press, 1973. 48 pp. (0-521-20228-0 pb.) Junior-Senior.

Born into a family of Christian Romans living in Britain at the end of the Roman Empire, Patrick spent six years as a slave in Ireland when he was a youth; later, when he became a priest, he was sent back to Ireland as a missionary. Interspersing Patrick's story with early Irish history, Corfe shows how Christianity was spread and how the great medieval Irish monasteries came into being. He discusses other Irish saints, missionaries to England and Europe, and the divide between Roman and Irish Catholicism. Black and white illustrations appear throughout the text, and some modern ones show the continuity of Irish Catholicism.

207. Fritz, Jean. *Brendan the Navigator: A History Mystery about the Discovery of America.* Illus. Enrico Arno. New York: Coward, McCann and Geoghegan, 1979. 32 pp. (0-698-20473-5 hc.) Elementary.

Did Brendan, the Irish saint, really cross the Atlantic in a leather boat in the sixth century? A medieval Latin text, *The Voyage of St. Brendan,* which may contain more fiction than fact, suggests he did. In her pleasing text, Fritz tells Brendan's life story, from joining a monastery as a youth, to performing miracles like ridding a village of fleas—and finally, to his voyage. Her Brendan is often bad-tempered, even when he encounters dragons or angels. Fritz ends with a note about Tim Severin's 1976 replication of Brendan's journey. Arno's charming two-color illustrations appear on every page.

208. ———. *The Man Who Loved Books.* Illus. Trina Schart Hyman. New York: Putnam's, 1981. 48 pp. (0-399-20715-5 hc.) Elementary.

This biography of St. Columba is illustrated with appealing pictures and Celtic designs in shades of brown. Fritz includes Columba's pet crane, his fight with Finian in which 3,000 men died over a book, and his settlement of the feud between the Irish bards and the king. Brief author's note.

209. Harrison, Cora. *The Viking at Drumshee*. Dublin: Wolfhound Press, 2001. 128 pp. (0-863-27788-8 pb.) Middle.
After a battle between the Vikings and the Irish, Conn, a 14-year-old boy in Brian Boru's tenth-century army—which is hard-pressed and out of food—captures Ivar, a Viking boy. Eventually, Conn, his sister, and Ivar become friends.

210. Llywelyn, Morgan. *Brian Boru: Emperor of the Irish*. 1990. New York: TOR Books, 1997. 192 pp. (0-312-85623-7 hc.) Junior-Senior.
Llywelyn retells the story of a historical figure in this novel. When his mother is killed by Vikings when he is a child, Brian Boru vows revenge. He spends time in a monastery learning to write—as well as to fight. Eventually he becomes the first high king of Ireland, uniting warring clans to defend their country against Viking attacks in the 10th and 11th centuries.

211. Stolz, Mary, writer/illus. *Pangur Ban*. New York: HarperCollins, 1988. 182 pp. (0-06-025862-4 hc.) Junior.
In ninth-century Ireland, lazy Cormac, the 14-year-old son of a farmer, wants to be an artist. His father finally gives him to a monastery where he can work in the scriptorium, and his cat, Pangur Ban, accompanies him. Seventeen years later Vikings attack the monastery. Stolz bases her delightful novel on the medieval Irish poem about a scribe and his cat and her illustrations imitate medieval Irish manuscript designs.

Anglo-Saxon England

The Anglo-Saxon period can be said to have taken place between the 5th and 11th centuries. In the 5th century, the Roman legions who had outposts in England withdrew as the Roman Empire disintegrated. At roughly the same time, Germanic tribes (especially the Angles, Saxons, and Jutes) began invading Britain, looking for places to settle. The British people who were already living there, many of whom had accepted Roman ways and Roman Catholicism, resisted, but in the end, it was the pagan Germanic tribes who prevailed.

Their language, known as both Old English and Anglo-Saxon, took precedence over the Celtic languages like Welsh that had been spoken in Britain. Although Welsh survives, only a few words from that language were adopted into Old English. Even the name used for the surviving British natives demonstrates the overwhelming dominance of the Anglo-Saxons; "Welsh" is from an Old English word meaning foreigner.

Ironically, once they began to think of themselves as English, the Anglo-Saxons themselves suffered from invasions by more Germanic people from Europe: the Vikings began to raid and settle England in the ninth century. King Alfred the Great fought them, finally establishing a treaty that defined the north of England as the Danelaw, or the area controlled by the Danish settlers.

Two centuries later, Anglo-Saxon England drew to a close in yet another invasion. William the Conqueror's Norman army won not only a military victory, but in some ways a linguistic one. Just as the Anglo-Saxons brought their Germanic language to England in the fifth and sixth centuries, William introduced the French language and French cultural and political ideas to the land. However, while Old English completely subsumed the Celtic languages, William the Conqueror's French did not force Old English out of existence. Instead, it influenced the English language greatly, and what had been Old English became Middle English.

Many writers have been inspired by these three times of turmoil in Anglo-Saxon England: the Germanic invasions of the 5th century, King Alfred's struggles with the Danes in the 9th century, and Harold Godwinson's loss to William the Conqueror in the 11th century. Another topic that draws writers' attention is the coming of Christianity to Anglo-Saxon England, especially St. Augustine's arrival in Canterbury in 597. And finally, many writers have found ways to weave Anglo-Saxon literature into their works.

Nonfiction

212. Coote, Roger. *The Anglo-Saxons*. Look into the Past Series. New York: Thomson Learning, 1994. 32 pp. (1-568-47062-2 lib. bdg.) Elementary-Middle.

Using mostly double-page spreads with excellent photos of artifacts (jewelry, coins, buildings, weapons, and a reconstructed Anglo-Saxon village), as well as photos of manuscript illustrations, the book is divided into short introductory paragraphs followed by more detailed paragraphs keyed to specific illustrations. This is a solid introduction for readers who want to know what the Anglo-Saxons ate and wore and how they farmed, fought, and prayed. Glossary, time line, further reading, index.

213. Crossley-Holland, Kevin. *Green Blades Rising: The Anglo-Saxons.* New York: Seabury Press, 1976. 143 pp. (0-816-43154-X hc.) Junior-Senior.

Using literature and visual arts, including architecture, jewelry, and manuscripts, Crossley-Holland explores the physical and cultural lives of the Anglo-Saxons. Index, bibliography.

214. Hodges, C. Walter. *The Norman Conquest.* New York: Coward-McCann, 1966. 32 pp. Elementary.

An explanation of the political events and the battle of 1066, illustrated in color.

215. Lace, William W. *The Battle of Hastings.* San Diego: Lucent Books, 1996. 96 pp. (1-560-06416-1 lib. bdg.) Junior-Senior.

This detailed account begins with a chapter on early British history, the coming of the Anglo-Saxons, and the reign of Alfred the Great, in order to set the stage for the Norman Conquest. Lace explains the complicated politics of 11th-century England, Normandy, and Scandinavia before he dives into the story of William and Harold, and finally the battle itself. Maps, insets with quotations, black and white illustrations from the Bayeux Tapestry, and 19th-century engravings (annoyingly not identified as such) illustrate the text. Chronology, further reading, bibliography, index.

216. Triggs, Tony D. *The Saxons.* 1979. New York: Silver Burdett, 1980. 61 pp. (0-382-06359-7 lib. bdg.) Middle-Junior.

Double-page spreads illustrated with paintings and a few photos detail Anglo-Saxon history, daily life, agriculture, law, religion, literature, art, and crafts. A few stories and poems are excerpted, and *Beowulf* is summarized. A final time line places the Anglo-Saxons in the context of other world cultures. Glossary, index.

Fiction

217. Alder, Elizabeth. *The King's Shadow*. New York: Farrar, Straus & Giroux, 1995. 259 pp. (0-440-22011-4 pb.) Junior.

In the years leading up to 1066, Evyn, a Welsh boy who wanted to become a bard until ruffians cut his tongue out, is sold into slavery. His fortunes rise as he follows King Harold Godwinson and eventually becomes his foster son. Alder skillfully incorporates parts of *The Song of Roland*, *Beowulf*, and *The Anglo-Saxon Chronicle* into the novel, and she portrays late Anglo-Saxon England responsibly.

218. Crossley-Holland, Kevin. *Wulf*. Illus. Gareth Floyd. London: Faber and Faber, 1988. 112 pp. (0-571-15100-0 hc.) Junior.

In seventh-century East Anglia, Wulf is a young boy who comes to know the missionary Cedd at a time when the Anglo-Saxons are converting to Christianity. This book is a reworking of an earlier trilogy, *The Sea-Stranger* (London: Heinemann, 1973); *The Fire-Brother* (1975); and *The Earth-Father* (1976).

219. Cumberlege, Vera. *The Grey Apple Tree*. Illus. Victor Ambrus. London: Andre Deutsch, 1965. Middle.

In England in 1066, young John witnesses the Battle of Hastings. The book draws on an account of Horsted, a village that is described in *Domesday Book*, William the Conqueror's account of his holdings in England.

220. Henty, G. A. *The Dragon and the Raven, or The Days of King Alfred*. 1886. London, Ontario: Althouse Press, 2002. 368 pp. (1-590-87120-0 pb.) Junior.

In 870, Edmund, a young member of the nobility, takes part in King Alfred's battles against the Danes. Several other editions of this book exist, including an audio version performed by John Bolen.

221. ———. *Wulf the Saxon: A Story of the Norman Conquest*. 1894. Mill Hall, PA: Preston Speed Publications, 1998. 361 pp. (1-887-15920-7 pb.) Junior.

Wulf is a young nobleman who fights at the side of Harold Godwinson in his wars against the Welsh, against the Danes at the Battle of Stamford Bridge, and, finally, against the Normans at the Battle of Hastings in 1066. Wulf is accompanied by his best friend Beorn and his servant Osgood.

222. Hodges, C. Walter, writer/illus. *The Marsh King*. New York: Coward-McCann, 1967. 255 pp. Junior-Senior.
In this sequel to *The Namesake*, the unnamed narrator vows to write down the events of his grandfather's and mother's time, when King Alfred the Great fought the Danes. The narrator interweaves stories of his fictional family, especially his mother Hildis, with historical and legendary events of the ninth century, including the tale of King Alfred burning the cakes in the peasant woman's cottage. Black and white illustrations every few chapters give a good view of Anglo-Saxon clothing and ornament.

223. ———. *The Namesake*. 1964. New York: Coward-McCann, 1967. 271 pp. Junior-Senior.
Alfred the One-Legged looks back on his life as a scribe to King Alfred the Great. Having lost a leg in childhood during the Danish invasions, he is brought up in a monastery and later becomes part of King Alfred the Great's household. The king asks him to learn to read and write so he can be his secretary and scribe. But times are hard, because the Danes continue to harry the Saxons, and it takes all of King Alfred's strength and cunning to fashion a peace with them. Carnegie Commendation.

224. Lewis, Hilda. *Harold Was My King*. 1968. New York: McKay, 1970. 246 pp. Junior.
In 11th-century England, just after the Norman Conquest, a young steward who had served as King Harold's page before the king was killed in the Battle of Hastings refuses to accept the rule of William the Conqueror.

225. McGraw, Eloise. *The Striped Ships*. New York: Macmillan, 1991. 229 pp. (0-689-50532-9 hc.) Middle-Junior.
Juliana, the teenaged daughter of an Anglo-Saxon aristocrat, sees a reversal of her fortunes when the Normans invade England in 1066. In order to survive, she finds a job in Canterbury, where her younger brother is a novice at a monastery, helping the embroiderers of the Bayeux Tapestry. McGraw's depiction of a society in turmoil is impressive; Juliana is a strong female character who does not seem anachronistically modern.

226. Schouten, Alet. *Flight into Danger*. Illus. Bill Greer. New York: Random House, 1972. 176 pp. (0-394-92283-2 lib. bdg.) Junior.
In the ninth century a young slave escapes to the Low Countries from Britain.

227. Sutcliff, Rosemary. *Dawn Wind*. Illus. Charles Keeping. 1961. New York: Henry Z. Walck, 1962. 241 pp. Junior-Senior.
In sixth-century Britain 14-year-old Owain and his dog are the only survivors of a battle against the invading Saxons. He befriends Regina, a 12-year-old beggar, and the two struggle to survive. When Regina becomes ill, Owain sells himself into slavery to save her. He lives with the Saxons for eleven years before earning his freedom in 597, the year he witnesses the missionary St. Augustine landing in England.

228. ———. *The Shining Company*. New York: Farrar, Straus & Giroux / Sunburst, 1992. 295 pp. (0-374-46616-5 pb.) Junior-Senior.
Around the year 600, in the generations after the Roman legions have withdrawn from England, and in the time of the Germanic invasions, 12-year-old Prosper, the son of a British chieftain, is a shield bearer to one of the 300 Companions sung about in the *Gododdin*, an early British poem. They go to Dyn Eidin—later Edinburgh—to prepare for the fight against the Saxons. Author's note, pronunciation guide. BBYA, ALA Notable Children's Book.

229. Tingle, Rebecca. *The Edge on the Sword*. New York: Putnam's, 2001. 288 pp. (0-399-23580-9 hc.) Junior-Senior.
In the late 800s, 15-year-old Æthelflæd, daughter of King Alfred the Great, learns to ride and fight from the bodyguard who is to take her to her new husband. The accurate historical details and inclusion of Old English literature add to the richness of this novel about a real woman who became an Anglo-Saxon military leader. Historical note. BBYA.

230. Trease, Geoffrey. *Escape to King Alfred*. (British title: *Mist over Athelney*.) New York: Vanguard, 1958. 251 pp. Middle-Junior.
In southwestern England in 878, two children escape their Danish captors and make an arduous journey to find King Alfred and warn him of the Danes' plans to break their treaty and attack. They hide with the king and his family in the forest and help him fight his decisive battle against Guthrum.

231. Treece, Henry. *Hounds of the King*. Illus. Christine Price. London: Bodley Head, 1955. 155 pp. Middle-Junior.

As a child, Beornoth swears an oath to Harold Godwinson. Later he becomes one of Harold's chosen warriors, the Housecarles, and fights alongside him at the Battle of Hastings, where Harold is killed. Glossary.

232. ———. *The Invaders: Three Stories*. Illus. Charles Keeping. Intro. Margery Fisher. New York: Thomas Y. Crowell, 1972. 120 pp. (0-690-4493-3 hc.) Middle-Junior.

These stories span the period from the end of Roman Britain to the end of Anglo-Saxon England. The first is about a Roman soldier and a British tribal leader. In the second, Vikings attack England, and in the third, a follower of Harold Godwinson's tries unsuccessfully to kill William the Conqueror.

233. ———. *Man with a Sword*. Illus. William Stobbs. 1962. New York: Pantheon, 1964. 244 pp. Junior-Senior.

As Treece explains in an introduction, the story takes place in the years 1041–1087. England may be its main setting, but because of the complex political machinations of the times, the action is wide-ranging, touching "on events in Flanders, Denmark, Norway, Constantinople, England, and Normandy." Hereward the Wake, who refused to accept William's rule of England, is the protagonist.

234. Tully, J. *The Raven and the Cross*. Illus. Derek Collard. London: BBC, 1974. Middle-Junior.

During the Viking raids, young Edwina warns King Alfred about their presence after they kill her father, a nobleman.

235. Walsh, Jill Paton, and Kevin Crossley-Holland. *Wordhoard: Anglo-Saxon Stories*. New York: Farrar, Straus & Giroux, 1969. 160 pp. Junior-Senior.

These eight thoughtful, intelligent stories (four by each author) take place throughout the Anglo-Saxon era. The first is about the Saxon invasions of England, and the last, about King Harold at the Battle of Hastings, is set at the very end of Anglo-Saxon England. Several are inspired by Anglo-Saxon literature: one tells about King Alfred and Asser, his biographer; another features Ælfric, whose *Colloquy* helped young novices learn their Latin; another recalls Cædmon's meeting with Abbess Hild.

236. Willard, Barbara. *Augustine Came to Kent.* 1964. Illus. Mary Beth
    Owens. Warsaw, ND: Bethlehem Books, 1997. 179 pp. (1-883-
    93721-3 pb.) Middle-Junior.
In the year 597, Wolf and his father accompany St. Augustine on his
mission to England. Wolf's father, a British slave in Rome, was freed by
Pope Gregory and sent back to his homeland. They witness the meeting between Augustine and the king of Kent.

Beowulf
Although *Beowulf* is an epic poem about a legendary hero who fights
monsters, books based on it appear here, rather than with medieval legends, because the poem is so closely associated with Anglo-Saxon England. Ironically, however, the events it describes are set in Scandinavia, not England. Hrothgar, whose hall is being ravaged by the
monster Grendel, is Danish, while Beowulf comes from another Scandinavian people, the Geats. The legendary events of the poem would
have taken place before the Germanic tribes began their migrations to
England in the fifth century. Yet the language of the poem is Old English, and the only surviving manuscript is from tenth-century England.

237. Crossley-Holland, Kevin. *Beowulf.* Illus. Charles Keeping. 1982.
    Oxford: Oxford University Press, 1999. 46 pp. (0-192-72369-3 hc.)
    Junior-Senior.
An abridgement of the 1968 poetic translation published by Farrar,
Straus & Giroux. Crossley-Holland uses both alliteration and caesuras
within lines, but without forcing either poetic aspect.

238. Hosford, Dorothy. *By His Own Might: The Battles of Beowulf.* Illus.
    Laszlo Matulay. New York: Henry Holt, 1947. 69 pp. Junior-Senior.
This prose retelling, divided into ten chapters and illustrated with
black and white woodcuts, follows the original closely.

239. Nye, Robert. *Beowulf: A New Telling.* Illus. Alan E. Cober. 1968.
    New York: Dell, 1982. 94 pp. (0-440-90560 pb.) Junior.
This unimpressive prose "interpretation" includes many scenes from
Nye's imagination, including a battle between Hrothgar and Grendel,
Unferth's alliance with Grendel, and Beowulf's use of bees to defeat the
dragon.

240. Serrailler, Ian. *Beowulf the Warrior*. Illus. Severin. 1954. New York: Henry Z. Walck, 1961. 48 pp. Junior.

This verse translation removes the digressions and focuses on Beowulf's three battles: with Grendel, Grendel's mother, and the dragon. The verse uses some alliteration, four beats to the line, and a caesura in each line. Stylized black and white illustrations incorporate Anglo-Saxon interlace designs. Reprinted in 1994 by Bethlehem Books.

241. Sutcliff, Rosemary. *Dragon Slayer: The Story of Beowulf*. (Alternate title: *Beowulf*.) 1961. Illus. Charles Keeping. New York: Penguin, 1966. 108 pp. (0-14-030254-9 pb.) Middle-Junior.

The story is retold as a novel, fleshed out with physical and psychological details. It begins with Beowulf hearing the story of Grendel and knowing that he must help King Hrothgar, who had once helped his father. Some events are made more realistic; for example, the swimming match with Breca becomes a walrus-hunting match, undertaken in boats, when Beowulf tells the story. Yet the fantastic elements of the poem remain in place when he fights the monsters.

CHAPTER SIX

British Isles, 1066–1500

This chapter focuses on the high and late Middle Ages, from just after the Norman Conquest of England in the 11th century through the end of the medieval period. The Normans brought not only the French language with them to England, but also French ideas about social and political structures, like feudalism and chivalry. Fashions in clothing, in literature, even in conduct changed, and they kept changing from the high to the late Middle Ages. Despite the variety of experience during this period of over four hundred years, there was some continuity. First, the Roman Catholic Church defined people's lives in large and small ways. Secondly, the entire medieval period can be characterized as a manuscript age, a time when all books had to be copied by hand in a laborious and time-consuming process. William Caxton's introduction of moveable type to England in 1476 was a technological change as sweeping as the computer revolution of the 20th century. In an introduction to his first printed edition, Caxton remarks that instead of being written with pen and ink the way books usually are, all of the copies of his history of Troy were begun and finished *in the same day*. This technological marvel and the cultural ideas sweeping in from Italy, where the Renaissance had already begun, were just two of the signals that the medieval period was ending.

The books in this section illustrate some of the changes that were taking place throughout this period. In literature, we see the beginnings of medieval drama, followed by Chaucer making English an acceptable language for court literature in the 14th century. Politically, the tension between church and state is played out in the fraught relationship between Henry II and Thomas Becket, and many writers have been inspired by Becket's murder, and by the later events of the Hundred Years' War between England and France, especially Henry V's decisive 15th-century victory at Agincourt. Socially, the rise of towns, the merchant classes, and the powerful guilds provide choice subjects for fiction writers.

Nonfiction

242. Childress, Diana. *Chaucer's England.* North Haven, CT: Linnet Books, 2000. 137 pp. (0-208-02489-1 hc.) Junior-Senior.
A very readable text distinguishes this introduction to 14th-century England. It covers political and social structures, medieval learning, and daily life and includes good black and white illustrations, all from medieval sources. Bibliography, further reading, index.

243. Chrisp, Peter. *The Normans.* Look into the Past Series. 1994. New York: Thomson Learning, 1995. 32 pp. (1-56847-174-2 hc.) Elementary-Middle.
Although the Normans' origins among the Vikings and their travels into Italy are mentioned, the focus is on William's conquest of England. Fittingly, many of the illustrations are from the Bayeux Tapestry, and others are from manuscript and church art as well as photos. Short paragraphs accompany the excellent illustrations. Glossary, time line, further reading, index.

244. Corfe, Tom. *Archbishop Thomas and King Henry II.* Cambridge Topic Books. Cambridge: Cambridge University Press, 1975. 48 pp. (0-521-206460-6 pb.) Junior-Senior.
Corfe begins with eyewitness accounts of Becket's murder inside Canterbury Cathedral before backtracking to explain the political and religious situation that led to it. Black and white photos and illustrations are well-integrated into the text, which is full of fascinating details

about monasteries, education, and even financial history. The book ends with a short chapter about the aftermath of the murder and the legacy of St. Thomas—including the 20th-century literary legacy.

245. Daugherty, James, writer/illus. *The Magna Charta.* New York: Random House, 1956. 181 pp. Junior.

In short chapters, Daugherty introduces the most negative aspects of 12th-century life, like torture and servitude, before shifting his focus to King John's youth and reign. English political history comes to life with personalities, but Daugherty's facts are sometimes wanting. For example, he presents Robin Hood and his Merry Men as historical, not legendary, figures. In his last chapter, "Children of the Magna Charta," he writes about American charters, including the Mayflower Compact, the Declaration of Independence, the Fifteenth Amendment, and the charter of the United Nations. Index.

246. Duggan, Alfred. *Growing Up with the Norman Conquest.* Illus. C. Walter Hodges. 1965. New York: Pantheon, 1966. 217 pp. Junior-Senior.

In five substantial narrative chapters, Duggan tells about the lives of various groups in Norman England—a baron's family, a freeman's family, city dwellers, children brought up to the religious life, and peasants. For each group, he invents characters and follows their days, providing a great deal of social and cultural context. A few black and white sketches accompany each chapter. Index.

247. Green, Robert. *William the Conqueror.* New York: Franklin Watts, 1998. 64 pp. (0-531-20353-0 lib. bdg.) Elementary-Middle.

An eye-catching cover and some good interior reproductions of medieval artwork may draw readers to this book, and the well-written prose will keep them reading this account of William's life and battles. Further reading, Internet sources, genealogy, index.

248. Hamley, Dennis. *Three Towneley Plays.* The Kingswood Plays for Boys and Girls Series. London: Heinemann Educational Books, 1962. 77 pp. Junior-Senior.

Hamley adapts three works from the medieval English miracle play cycles, performed by the guilds, into modern English: *The Play of the Killing of Abel*, *The Play of Noah and His Son*, and *The First Shepherd's*

Play. In his introduction, he explains the history of medieval drama and discusses the performances of miracle plays.

249. Hodges, C. Walter, writer/illus. *Magna Carta.* New York: Coward-McCann, 1966. 32 pp. Elementary-Middle.
Through watercolors and a straightforward text, Hodges helps readers understand the grim facts of peasant life, the venality of nobles, and the succession of rulers who led up to the Magna Carta. Keeping his focus mainly on royalty, from King Stephen to King John, he explains the political situation and the people involved, including the murder of Thomas Becket during Henry II's reign. Although it is designed like a picture book, many of the ideas within the text are complex.

250. Lace, William W. *Little Princes in the Tower.* Mysterious Deaths Series. San Diego: Lucent Books, 1996. 112 pp. (1-560-06262-2 lib. bdg.) Junior-Senior.
Were Crown Prince Edward and his younger brother murdered by Richard III? Nobody knows, but they were imprisoned and disappeared under mysterious circumstances during the Hundred Years' War. That's the story Lace tells here, and he does a good job of explaining the complex political situation that led to the boys' deaths. Inset paragraphs tell about people, events, and social customs, quote from primary sources, and define terms; black and white photos and reproductions further illustrate the text.

251. Serraillier, Ian. *Chaucer and His World.* New York: Henry Z. Walck, 1967. 48 pp. (0-8098-3075-2 hc.) Junior-Senior.
Beginning with a short biography of the poet, this solid little book gives details of what the lives of the Canterbury pilgrims would have been like. Quotations from the poem are used throughout the text. The black and white illustrations from medieval sources are well-captioned.

252. Tanaka, Shelley. *In the Time of the Knights: The Real-Life History of History's Greatest Knight.* Illus. Greg Ruhl. I Was There Series. New York: Hyperion, 2000. 48 pp. (0-786-80651-6 hc.) Middle.
This biography of William Marshal, the 12th-century English knight, adds fictional elements to flesh out the undocumented parts of Marshal's life, but Tanaka also draws on the historical record. Maps, medieval art, color photos, and contemporary illustrations enhance the tale.

253. Weatherly, Myra S. *William Marshal: Medieval England's Greatest Knight*. British Heroes Series. Greensboro, NC: Morgan Reynolds, 2001. 112 pp. (1-883-84648-X hc.) Middle-Junior.

Black and white illustrations, maps, genealogical tables, and side notes about life in medieval Europe supplement this biography of William Marshal, who served many royals, including a stint as Eleanor of Aquitaine's bodyguard. Although the focus is on Marshal, the book is a good introduction to 12th-century English and European political and court life.

Fiction

254. Avi. *Crispin: The Cross of Lead*. New York: Hyperion, 2002. 262 pp. (0-7868-0828-4 hc.) Middle.

In 1377, an orphaned peasant boy is falsely accused of murder and finds refuge with a traveling entertainer, who is secretly involved with John Ball. Avi uses historical details skillfully, letting them illuminate but not overshadow Crispin's exciting adventures. Newbery Medal.

255. Bibby, Violet. *The Mirrored Shield*. Illus. Graham Humphreys. London: Longman Young Books, 1970. 145 pp. Middle.

In 15th-century Canterbury, young Thomas is raised by an herbalist, but when his talent for carving is discovered, he finds work with the Master Mason.

256. Branford, Henrietta. *Fire, Bed & Bone*. Cambridge, MA: Candlewick, 1998. 122 pp. (0-7636-0338-4 hc.) Middle-Junior.

When her masters, an English peasant family, are thrown into jail on suspicion of being involved in the 1381 Peasants' Revolt, it is left to an old hunting dog to tell their story—and her own. Despite the canine perspective, life in a late medieval village is clearly evoked.

257. Carrick, Donald, writer/illus. *Harald and the Giant Knight*. New York: Clarion, 1982. 32 pp. (0-89919-060-X hc.) Elementary.

In feudal England, a group of knights threatens Harald's parents' farm by practicing for a tournament on their fields and eating their poultry. Harald thinks up a plan to frighten the knights away, and he and his parents carry it out. The illustrations—large, double-page spreads—indicate Carrick's familiarity with his subject.

258. ———. *Harald and the Great Stag*. New York: Clarion, 1988. 32 pp. (0-89919-514-8 lib. bdg.) Elementary.
Young Harald risks his life in a plausible ploy to save a stag when the baron and his men come to the forest to hunt it. Each double-page spread boasts a splendid watercolor full of fascinating period detail; readers will learn even more about medieval hunting from the illustrations than they will from the short text.

259. Clarke, Pauline. *The Boy with the Erpingham Hood*. Illus. Cecil Leslie. London: Faber and Faber, 1956. 223 pp. Junior.
A boy from Norfolk goes to Agincourt with his lord. Later he becomes a mason.

260. Cushman, Karen. *Catherine, Called Birdy*. New York: Clarion, 1994. 170 pp. (0-395-68186-3 hc.) Middle-Junior.
thirteen-year-old Catherine, the only daughter of the lord of an English manor, keeps a diary of the year 1290, during which she resists her father's attempts to marry her off. In general, Cushman does a wonderful job of evoking medieval life by focusing on fascinating details and using humor to good effect. Author's note. Newbery Honor, BBYA, ALA Notable Children's Book.

261. ———. *Matilda Bone*. New York: Clarion, 2000. 176 pp. (0-395-88156-0 hc.) Middle-Junior.
In a 14th-century English town, Matilda, brought up among the aristocracy by a priest, suddenly finds herself living with Red Peg the Bonesetter and expected to take part in middle-class life—even to get her hands dirty. Slowly, she begins to appreciate the people around her and to learn the value of practical medicine, not just book learning. Author's note.

262. ———. *The Midwife's Apprentice*. New York: Clarion, 1995. 128 pp. (0-395-69229-6 hc.) Middle-Junior.
Homeless Alyce insinuates herself into the midwife's home, learning her trade and finding a place for herself in a 13th-century English village. Author's note. Newbery Medal.

263. De Angeli, Marguerite, writer/illus. *The Door in the Wall*. 1949. New York: Doubleday, 1989. 111 pp. (0-385-07283-X pb.) Middle.

In London in the year 1325, Robin is expected to become a page, but he gets sick and loses the use of his legs. A kindly monk looks after him and Robin learns to care for others, not just himself. Newbery Medal.

264. French, Allen. *The Lost Baron: A Story of England in the Year 1200*. Illus. Andrew Wyeth. 1940. Bathgate, ND: Bethlehem Books, 2001. 247 pp. (1-883-93753-1 pb.) Middle-Junior.

In Cornwall, 13-year-old Martin is supposed to serve as a page to Baron Eric. But on Martin's first day in service, the baron disappears and his heir, the frightening Sir Basil, takes over. Martin is thrust into matters of intrigue and justice.

265. Goodman, Joan Elizabeth. *Peregrine*. Boston: Houghton Mifflin, 2000. 228 pp. (0-395-97729-0 hc.) Junior.

In 1144 the 15-year-old widow Lady Edith goes on a pilgrimage from England to Jerusalem. Although much of the medieval setting is accurate, Edith meets Margery Kempe, a 15th-century woman, during her travels, as well as an improbable runaway Welsh princess who communicates telepathically. Will Belet, from *The Winter Hare*, plays a role. Author's note.

266. ———. *The Winter Hare*. Boston: Houghton Mifflin, 1996. 255 pp. (0-395-78569-3 hc.) Junior.

In England in 1140, during the anarchy of King Stephen, 12-year-old Will Belet serves as a page at his uncle's castle and becomes involved in dangerous political maneuverings, based on events described in *The Peterborough Chronicle*. He helps Empress Matilda escape imprisonment. Will appears again in *Peregrine*. Author's note.

267. Gray, Elizabeth Janet. *Adam of the Road*. Illus. Robert Lawson. New York: Viking, 1942. 320 pp. (0-670-10435-3 pb.) Middle-Junior.

In 1294, 11-year-old Adam, traveling with his father, Roger the Minstrel, and his beloved dog Nick, loses them both and undertakes a long journey to find them. His adventures take him through southeastern England, from a robber's lair to a fair at Winchester, to London and St. Albans, and finally to Oxford. This gentle story is filled with fascinating details about medieval England. Newbery Medal.

268. Haahr, Berit. *The Minstrel's Tale*. New York: Delacorte, 2000. 272 pp. (0-385-32713-7 hc.) Middle-Junior.

In this adventure romance with medieval trappings, a 13-year-old girl runs away from home to avoid marrying a much older man. She dresses as a boy, joins a group of minstrels, and falls in love.

269. Hamley, Dennis. *Pageants of Despair*. New York: S. G. Phillips, 1974. 175 pp. (0-87599-205-6 hc.) Junior.
A 20th-century boy time-travels to 15th-century England and becomes involved in the performance of miracle plays. Hamley uses his knowledge of medieval drama and weaves historical figures in with fictional ones. This is more of a fantasy than historical fiction—for example, the actors transform into the characters they are playing—but it does portray the miracle plays accurately. Author's note with bibliography.

270. Harnett, Cynthia, writer/illus. *The Cargo of the Madalena*. (British title: *The Load of the Unicorn*; alternate title: *Caxton's Challenge*.) 1959. Minneapolis: Lerner, 1984. 236 pp. (0-8225-0890-7 hc.) Junior.
In London in the 1470s, William Caxton has set up his printing press. Bendy's family are scribes whose livelihood is threatened by this new technology. Bendy himself secretly admires Caxton, and he finds himself torn when his brothers hatch a plot against the printer. Carnegie Commendation.

271. ———. *The Merchant's Mark*. (British title: *The Wool Pack*; alternate title: *Nicholas and the Wool Pack*.) 1953. Minneapolis: Lerner, 1984. 183 pp. (0-8225-0891-5 hc.) Junior.
In the Cotswolds in the 1490s, 15-year-old Nicholas is being trained to become a wool merchant like his father. His father has also betrothed him to Cecily, a girl he has never met. When Italian merchants threaten his father's business, it falls to Nicholas and Cecily to save the day. Carnegie Medal.

272. ———. *The Sign of the Green Falcon*. (Alternate titles: *Ring Out, Bow Bells*; *The Drawbridge Gate*.) 1953. Minneapolis: Lerner, 1984. 288 pp. (0-8225-0888-5 hc.) Junior.
In London in 1415, Dickon wants to become a grocer, but instead is apprenticed to his godfather, the wool merchant and mayor Dick Whittington. He unwittingly becomes involved in a plot against King Henry V.

273. ———. *The Writing on the Hearth.* Illus. Gareth Floyd. 1971. Minneapolis: Lerner, 1984. 300 pp. (0-8225-0889-3 hc.) Junior.
In Suffolk in 1439, during the childhood of Henry VI, Stephen wants to study at Oxford, but he fears he may not be able to when people connect him with a practitioner of black magic.

274. Hendry, Frances. *Quest for a Maid.* New York: Farrar, Straus & Giroux, 1992. 273 pp. (0-374-46155-4 hc.) Middle-Junior.
In the 13th century, during a time of tension over who the rightful ruler of Scotland is, Meg is betrothed to the son of Sir Patrick Spens. She goes on a sea journey to Norway to bring back an eight-year-old girl, the rightful queen of Scotland. More an adventure romance infused with history than a historical novel, the book includes witchcraft (Meg's older sister is a witch). ALA Notable Book.

275. Henty, G. A. *In Freedom's Cause: A Story of Wallace and Bruce.* 1885. New York: Dover Publications, 2002. 320 pp. (0-486-42362-X pb.) Middle-Junior.
In 14th-century Scotland young Archibald Forbes becomes involved in the struggle for Scottish freedom from England, led by William Wallace and Robert the Bruce. Archibald twice saves the life of Wallace and is present at the Battle of Bannockburn in 1314.

276. ———. *St. George for England: A Tale of Cressy and Poitiers.* Illus. Frank Gilett. 1885. Mill Hall, PA: Preston Speed Publications, 2000. 290 pp. (1-887-15927-4 pb.) Middle-Junior.
During the Hundred Years' War, young Walter fights for the English at the battles of Crécy and Poitiers. He (and the reader along with him) sees some of the well-known people and events of the 14th century, including the Black Death and Edward the Black Prince.

277. Hunter, Mollie. *The King's Swift Rider: A Novel of Robert the Bruce.* New York: HarperCollins, 1998. 322 pp. (0-06-027186-8 pb.) Junior-Senior.
In 1292 in Scotland, 16-year-old Martin becomes a spy for Robert the Bruce—who fought with William Wallace—and his rebel army. Author's note.

278. Jewett, Eleanore M. *The Hidden Treasure of Glaston.* Illus. Frederick T. Chapman. 1947. Bathgate, ND: Bethlehem Books, 2000. 323 pp. (1-883-93748-5 pb.) Middle-Junior.

In 1171 after Thomas Becket's murder, young Hugh de Morville's father is exiled and Hugh, who is lame, is left at Glastonbury Abbey. He and his friend Dickon have adventures searching for King Arthur's grave. Author's note. Newbery Honor.

279. Jones, Terry. *The Knight and the Squire*. Illus. Michael Foreman. London: Pavilion, 1999. 288 pp. (1-862-05044-9 hc.) Middle-Junior.

Jones brings his Monty Python humor to his novel of Tom, a beguiling 14th-century English peasant boy, who ends up as a squire to a bumbling knight, fighting in France during the Hundred Years' War. His friend Alan, a true rascal, leads Tom into one hair-raising adventure after another. Although there is an element of fantasy in the book—Tom meets a wolfman who teaches him to communicate with wolves—Jones does a fine job of evoking medieval life. The narrator sometimes reminds readers of the differences between then and now, saying, for example, "Nobody would be inside watching television." Foreman's black and white sketches are a nice addition.

280. ———. *The Lady and the Squire*. Illus. Michael Foreman. London: Pavilion Books, 2000. 304 pp. (1-862-05417-7 hc.) Middle-Junior.

In this sequel to *The Knight and the Squire*, Tom and Alan—now revealed as Ann—join Emily, the young gentlelady of the title, who (like Ann) is escaping an unwelcome marriage. The book takes place in France, which the English are attacking. Like the first volume, this fast and funny book, with chapter titles like "How Tom Nearly Invented the Flushing Lavatory Five Hundred Years before Thomas Crapper," combines rollicking adventures with accurate details of medieval life. The ending paves the way for further volumes.

281. Kirwan, Anna. Girlhood Journeys: Book 1. *Juliet: A Dream Takes Flight*; England, 1339. Illus. Lynne Marshall. New York: Simon and Schuster, 1996. 71 pp. (0-689-80983-2 pb.) Elementary-Middle.

Marguerite, the daughter of the lord of the manor, and Juliet, the bailiff's daughter, are best friends. Marguerite worries about the man she will marry—but joyfully discovers her betrothed to be young, dashing, and handsome. With her family's approval, she asks Juliet to be her lady-in-waiting at court. Although ostensibly set in the 14th century, this is a costume drama that pays no attention to social realities. It is

the first in a lackluster series of three; each book ends with an adver-
tisement for dolls based on the characters.

282. ———. Girlhood Journeys: Book 2. *Juliet: Rescue at Marlehead Manor;
England, 1340.* Illus. Lynne Marshall. New York: Simon and Schuster,
1997. 71 pp. (0-689-80987-5 pb.) Elementary-Middle.
Now a lady-in-waiting to Marguerite, Juliet undertakes a dangerous
plan to get a message to a woman whose husband is falsely imprisoned
for treason.

283. ———. Girlhood Journeys: Book 3. *Juliet: Midsummer at Green-
chapel; England, 1340.* Illus. Lynne Marshall. New York: Simon and
Schuster, 1997. 72 pp. (0-689-81560-3 pb.) Elementary-Middle.
On Midsummer, when Juliet hopes to take part in the festivities, she instead must find the medicine for a sick falcon. Apparently mummy
powder is all that can heal it.

284. Lewis, Hilda. *The Gentle Falcon.* Illus. Evelyn Gibbs. 1952. New
York: Criterion, 1957. 256 pp. Junior.
In the 14th century, 15-year-old Isabella Clinton, who has been
brought up on an impoverished country manor, is chosen to become
lady-in-waiting to the 7-year-old French princess who will marry King
Richard II. Isabella becomes involved in court intrigues, always main-
taining her loyalty to her queen. The story also concerns Isabella's on-
off romance with Gilles Cobham, whose political leanings differ from
hers. Author's note.

285. ———. *Here Comes Harry.* Illus. William Stobbs. New York: Criterion, 1960. 261 pp. Junior.
Harry Rushden, whose father died fighting at Agincourt and whose
family has fallen on hard times, is ten when the future Henry VI is born
in 1421. After he becomes an apprentice goldsmith in London and
risks his life to save the four-year-old king, he becomes a spy for the
royal family. Author's note.

286. Llywelyn, Morgan. *Strongbow.* 1992. New York: TOR Books,
1997. 156 pp. (0-812-54462-5 pb.) Senior.
From alternating points of view, Llywelyn tells the story of the Norman
conquest of Ireland. The protagonists—Richard de Clare (called

Strongbow, he's a Norman knight) and Aoife, an Irish princess—have both lost their inheritance and seek to regain it. The book combines historical fiction with romance.

287. Love, D. Anne. *The Puppeteer's Apprentice*. New York: McElderry, 2003. 192 pp. (0-689-84424-7 hc.) Middle.

When her mistreatment becomes more than she can bear, 11-year-old Mouse runs away from the manor house where she works in the kitchen. She is fascinated with a puppet show she sees on the road, and through sheer perseverance and hard work, convinces the puppeteer to take her on as an apprentice. But the puppeteer has dark secrets that end up threatening Mouse. Bibliography and author's note about puppetry.

288. McCaughrean, Geraldine. *A Little Lower Than the Angels*. Oxford: Oxford University Press, 1988. 133 pp. (0-19-271561-5 hc.) Middle-Junior.

After he runs away from the cruel stonemason to whom he is apprenticed, Gabriel joins a band of traveling players. Because he looks so golden and innocent, he is cast as the angel in a mystery play. He doesn't just *look* innocent; it takes him a long time to understand that he is being used to help bilk people out of their money. The plague plays a role in this book, which sets it in the 14th century. It contains a fine portrayal of medieval drama. Whitbread Book of the Year.

289. Phillips, Ann. *The Peace Child*. New York: Oxford University Press, 1988. 150 pp. (0-19-271560-7 hc.) Middle.

In 14th-century England, two feuding families exchange children to bring about peace. One of them tells her story later, when her world is threatened by both plague and the 1381 Peasants' Revolt.

290. Picard, Barbara L. *Lost John: A Young Outlaw in the Forest of Arden*. Illus. Charles Keeping. 1962. New York: Criterion Books, 1963. 224 pp. Junior.

During the 12th-century reign of King John, a boy who is trying to avenge his father's death is captured by outlaws—the same outlaws who murdered his father.

291. ———. *One Is One*. Illus. Victor Ambrus. 1965. New York: Holt, 1966. 245 pp. Junior-Senior.

In 1318, Stephen, the son of a knight, battles himself: he is talented at drawing and could become a monk, but he wants to prove himself as a knight. This is an excellent depiction of life in a medieval monastery. Author's note. Carnegie Commendation.

292. ———. *Ransom for a Knight.* Illus. C. Walter Hodges. New York: Walck, 1967. 313 pp. Junior-Senior.

In a 20-month journey in 1315 after the Battle of Bannockburn, Lady Alys and Hugh, the son of a ploughman, carry the ransom for her father and brother from England to Scotland. This is a good portrayal of the class system. Carnegie Commendation.

293. Platt, Richard. *Castle Diary: The Journal of Tobias Burgess, Page.* Illus. Chris Riddell. Cambridge, MA: Candlewick, 1999. 64 pp. (0-7636-1584-6 pb.) Elementary-Middle.

The strength of this book is its comical illustrations of 11-year-old Toby and the other inhabitants, both nobles and peasants, of the fictional Strandborough Castle in the year 1285. There's more description than story as Toby spends a year being a page in his uncle's castle. Endnotes about "Toby's World" focus on warfare. Glossary, index.

294. Power, Rhoda. *Redcap Runs Away.* Illus. C. Walter Hodges. 1952. Boston: Houghton Mifflin, 1953. 303 pp. Middle-Junior.

In 14th-century England, Redcap, the son of a smith, runs away to join two minstrels. As they travel, they tell stories.

295. Pyle, Howard. *Men of Iron.* 1919. New York: Dover Publications, 2003. 190 pp. (0-486-42841-9 pb.) Middle-Junior.

Young Myles Falworth, in training to become a knight in 15th-century England, learns that his father has been falsely accused of treason by someone in power. It's up to Myles to regain his family's honor, despite the danger this puts him in. Pyle's adventure novel takes readers into castles and tournaments and illuminates some of the rigors of a knight's education.

296. Sancha, Sheila. *Knight after Knight.* 1974. New York: Walker, 1991. 208 pp. (0-744-51867-9 hc.) Junior.

In 14th-century England, knights didn't always get along, as this novel shows. Sir Bastion's father won't allow him to marry the girl he has chosen, while Sir Taxe is arrested when his castle is attacked.

297. Stevenson, Robert Louis. *The Black Arrow: A Tale of the Two Roses*. Illus. N. C. Wyeth. 1888. New York: Atheneum, 1987. 328 pp. (0-684-18877-5 lib. bdg.) Middle-Junior.

Hardly Stevenson's best work, this novel of adventure, love, friendship, and honor features plenty of outlaws, pirates, even a renegade priest. Its 16-year-old protagonist, Dick Shelton, wants to be a knight and he becomes enmeshed in the Wars of the Roses in late 15th-century England.

298. Sutcliff, Rosemary. *Knight's Fee*. Illus. Charles Keeping. New York: Henry Z. Walck, 1960. 241 pp. Junior-Senior.

Randal, an orphan who has taken care of the dogs in a Norman castle in Sussex, becomes the companion and eventually squire to Bevis, a knight's grandson. Despite their social differences, and the recognition that Randal cannot become a knight, he and Bevis become close friends.

299. ———. *The Witch's Brat*. Illus. Robert Micklewright. New York: Henry Z. Walck, 1970. 166 pp. Middle-Junior.

Lovel, a physically deformed 12th-century peasant, becomes a healer when he finds a place in a monastery. Eventually, he joins Rahere, the King's jongleur, and a historical character, as he builds St. Bartholomew's Hospital outside London. Sutcliff's impressive understanding of monastic life informs but never intrudes upon her portrayal of 12th-century England.

300. Temple, Frances. *The Ramsay Scallop*. New York: Orchard, 1994. 310 pp. (0-06-440601-6 pb.) Middle-Junior.

In 1299, 13-year-old Eleanor and Thomas, her betrothed, are sent on a pilgrimage from their English village to Santiago de Compostella in Spain. Along the way they come to know and love each other. They also meet many people—Christians, Muslims, and heretics—and hear many stories, like *The Chanson de Roland*, and Chaucer's *Clerk's Tale* and *Wife of Bath's Tale*. Eleanor's reactions to these stories and to the people she meets are those of a 20th-century girl; she is unconvincingly tolerant of religious diversity—and intolerant of medieval antifeminism. Also, differences in language are glossed over; everyone can understand everyone else along the pilgrimage route. BBYA.

301. Trease, Geoffrey. *The Baron's Hostage*. 1952. Revised ed. 1973. Nashville: T. Nelson, 1975. 160 pp. (0-840-76434-0 hc.) Middle-Junior.

In 13th-century England, a teenaged boy and girl—both noble—come to know each other. He is heir to a barony; she is a ward of the king and to be married for political purposes. In the background of their lives is the Barons' War (against Henry III), Simon de Montfort (who led the opposition to the king), and the birth of parliamentary rule.

302. ———. *The Red Towers of Granada*. Illus. Charles Keeping. New York: Vanguard Press, 1966. 185 pp. Junior.

In 1290 Robin, an English boy, is mistakenly diagnosed with leprosy and cast out of his village. Nor is he allowed to return to his studies in Oxford. He rescues a Jewish physician who heals him, but because he remains an outcast, unable to convince anyone that he has been healed, Robin leaves the country with Solomon and his family when the Jews are expelled from England. But Robin is actually undertaking a secret mission to find Spanish medicine for the queen. Medieval Spain is portrayed as a vibrant, multicultural society where Christians, Muslims, and Jews coexist peacefully and learning is valued.

303. ———. *Ride into Danger*. (British title: *The Bombard*.) Illus. Christine Price. New York: S. G. Phillips, 1959. 253 pp. (0-87599-113-0 hc.) Junior-Senior.

David Marlais, a proud 15-year-old from the Welsh Marches, who has both Norman and Welsh ancestry, is caught between the two warring cultures. When his father is wounded by a Welsh arrow, David goes to the king for permission to strengthen their manor. The king agrees, but only if David will accompany Edward the Black Prince to France. Thus, David ends up at the Battle of Crécy in 1346. After the fighting, he brings a bombard, an early cannon, back home with him to use against his Norman neighbors, but in doing so, he brings grief upon himself.

304. ———. *The Runaway Serf*. Illus. Mary Russon. 1966. London: Hamish Hamilton, 1975. 91 pp. Middle-Junior.

A peasant boy runs away from the manor on which he lives to the city of York, where he becomes an apprentice saddler.

305. ———. *The Secret Fiord*. Illus. Joe Krush. New York: Harcourt Brace, 1950. 241 pp. Junior.
Set in an English cathedral town, the plot involves a Corpus Christi play and an escape from Hanse merchants.

306. Turner, Ann. *The Way Home*. New York: Crown, 1982. 117 pp. (0-517-544261 hc.) Middle-Junior.
In 1349 in England, teenaged Anne escapes from her village when she is accused of bringing the plague because she has a harelip. She survives for months alone in the marshes before making the journey back. A man seeking a wife for his son kidnaps her, but again she escapes, only to find her entire village dead from the plague. Although Anne is a strong and resourceful protagonist, this is a less-than-convincing portrait of medieval England.

307. Wheeler, Thomas Gerald. *All Men Tall*. New York: S. G. Phillips, 1969. 256 pp. (87599-157-2 hc.) Junior.
For those interested in war and weapons, this old-fashioned novel, with its footnoted explanations, its maps, and its descriptions of battle, may appeal. In 14th-century England, the orphaned Thomeline serves at court until—marked for death—he escapes and joins Hugh the Armourer, who is working on the secret of gunpowder. Thomeline participates in the Battle of Crécy in 1346. Author's note.

308. Whitney, Elinor. *Tod of the Fens*. New York: Macmillan, 1928. 239 pp. Junior.
Although its didactic narrator and "forsoothy" language that owes more to Shakespeare than to Middle English—"Thou art no dull man," one character says—mark the book as old-fashioned, it can still be found on some library shelves. Tod is the rough master of a band of men who "lead a life of outdoor pleasure" in the fen country of 15th-century England, much like Robin Hood and his men. The crown prince disguised as a minstrel, a plot to steal a city's money, and a romance between two teenagers all lead, in the end, to Tod's elevation in society.

309. Willard, Barbara. *If All the Swords in England: A Story of Thomas Becket*. Illus. Robert M. Sax. 1961. Bathgate, ND: Bethlehem Books, 2000. 194 pp. (1-883-93749-3 pb.) Middle-Junior.

In 1170, twins Edmund and Simon, one a page to King Henry II and the other a scribe to Archbishop Thomas Becket, witness the tensions that result in Becket's death.

310. ———. *The Lark and the Laurel.* 1970. New York: Dell, 1989. 207 pp. (0-440-20156-X hc.) Junior-Senior.

The first of the eight Mantlemass novels (the series takes place between the death of Richard III and the end of the British Civil War, so most are postmedieval), this romance is set in 1485, against the backdrop of the Wars of the Roses. Mantlemass, the family estate in Sussex, is where Cecily Jolland goes unwillingly to live with her aunt when her father leaves for France. She changes her sheltered, pampered existence into one in which she learns to do for herself and to read. She grows to love her aunt and the people of Mantlemass, especially Lewis Mallory.

311. ———. *The Miller's Boy.* Illus. Gareth Floyd. New York: Dutton, 1976. 143 pp. (0-525-34970-7 hc.) Middle-Junior.

Thomas, a young boy in 15th-century Sussex, lives with his stern older sister and their crotchety grandfather, the miller. Thomas misses his married sister, Betsy, and he dearly wants a horse and a friend. Although he gets both, they bring trouble he never imagined when the friend he finds turns out to be of a considerably higher social class.

312. Williams, Laura. *The Executioner's Daughter.* New York: Henry Holt, 2000. 134 pp. (0-8050-6234-3 hc.) Middle.

Thirteen-year-old Lily, the daughter of a town's executioner, is destined to be her father's helper, and thus an outcast, until she runs away to become a healer. Ostensibly set in 1450 in England, this book gives readers little feel for the late medieval period. Author's note.

313. Williams, Ursula Moray. *The Noble Hawks.* (Alternate title: *The Earl's Falconer.*) London: Hamilton, 1959. 231 pp. Middle-Junior.

The son of a yeoman achieves his heart's desire: to become a falconer.

314. Yolen, Jane, and Robert Harris. *Girl in a Cage.* New York: Philomel, 2002. 256 pp. (0-399-23627-9 hc.) Middle-Junior.

In 1306, when Robert the Bruce becomes the contested King of Scotland, his 11-year-old daughter Marjorie is captured by King Edward of England and put in a cage on public display. This is the story of her twenty days of captivity. Author's note.

The Canterbury Tales

Chaucer's great unfinished cycle of stories in verse and prose, composed between 1380 and 1400, the year of his death, has long inspired writers. Below are a few of the retellings of his tales, some focused on a particular story, some a collection of several stories. A few other versions appear within anthologies of medieval legends in chapter 7.

315. Cohen, Barbara, adapter. *The Canterbury Tales*. Illus. Trina Schart Hyman. New York: Lothrop, Lee and Shepard, 1988. 88 pp. (0-688-06201-6 hc.) Elementary.

In her introduction, Cohen sets the scene at the Tabard Inn, and Hyman's illustrations portray and identify each of the pilgrims. The ones whose tales Cohen tells, in prose, are the Nun's Priest, the Pardoner, the Wife of Bath, and the Franklin, and she adapts their prologues, as well, to indicate where within the longer work they are situated. The details in the illustrations demonstrate Hyman's familiarity with Chaucer's writing.

316. Cooney, Barbara, adapter/illus. *Chanticleer and the Fox*. New York: Crowell, 1958. 36 pp. (0-690-18562-6 lib. bdg.) Elementary.

Cooney retells *The Nun's Priest's Tale* in prose, staying close to the original in her choice of words but leaving out all the material that doesn't contribute directly to the plot. Her simple, charming illustrations demonstrate her knowledge of both chickens and medieval life. Caldecott Medal.

317. Hastings, Selina, reteller. *A Selection from the Canterbury Tales*. Illus. Reg Cartwright. New York: Henry Holt, 1988. 77 pp. (0-8050-0904-3 hc.) Elementary.

Cleaning them up considerably (you'll find no farting here, and only coy references to sex) Hastings retells seven of Chaucer's tales: those of the Knight, Miller, Reeve, Nun's Priest, Pardoner, Wife of Bath, and Franklin. Each prose retelling begins with a few lines of description based on the General Prologue. Each tale gets several paintings: a portrait of the pilgrim, one full-page illustration, and a few smaller ones.

318. Lorenz, Lee. *Pinchpenny John*. Englewood Cliffs, NJ: Prentice-Hall, 1981. 32 pp. (0-13-676254-9 hc.) Elementary.

Lorenz, a *New Yorker* cartoonist, uses his familiar cartoon style to illustrate this book, which is "suggested by incidents in Chaucer's *The*

Miller's Tale." Here, however, John is Allison's grandfather, not her husband, and Nicholas wants to take Allison to the fair, not have sex with her—in order to steal John's gold. Absolon does not make it into Lorenz's version, but many other details from Chaucer's tale do. Nicholas turns out to be a scoundrel, and John learns to be less miserly. Lorenz has also retold *The Reeve's Tale* in picture-book form in *Scornful Simkin*.

319. McCaughrean, Geraldine. *The Canterbury Tales*. Illus. Victor Ambrus. 1984. Rand McNally, 1985. 120 pp. (0-516-09771-7 lib. bdg.) Elementary-Middle.

Chaucer uses a first-person narrator to tell his stories, and McCaughrean adopts that same pose in her prose retellings of twelve tales, plus a thirteenth in verse, the narrator's own poetic "Sir Thopas." (The poetry is so bad that the Host stops the narrator after a few verses.) She shortens, simplifies, and cleans up the tales considerably—there is no rape in the Wife of Bath's tale, no sex in the Reeve's or Merchant's, no farting in the Miller's—and she expands some of the matter between stories to emphasize personalities and relationships among the pilgrims. McCaughrean's pilgrims actually make it to Canterbury, and by the time they get there, the Host has become betrothed to the Wife of Bath.

320. Serraillier, Ian. *The Franklin's Tale*. Illus. Philip Gough. New York: Frederick Warne, 1972. 32 pp. (0-723-26092-3 hc.) Elementary.

Serraillier chooses prose to retell Chaucer's story of the squire who resorts to magic to try to win the love of a married woman.

CHAPTER SEVEN

Robin Hood

Whether the English hero Robin Hood really existed, we may never know. If he did, however, the outlawed archer associated with 12th-century Sherwood Forest would not have stolen from the rich to give to the poor; that aspect of the legend did not appear until the 16th century. In fact, in some medieval ballads, Robin and his men thoughtlessly kill villagers, servants, and children, making it no wonder that he is feared, not praised, by commoners in these tales. Stories of Robin Hood and his band of followers circulated in ballad form throughout the later Middle Ages and early modern period, gradually adding the characters and romantic situations so familiar to us from films and books like Howard Pyle's *The Merry Adventures of Robin Hood of Great Renown in Nottinghamshire*, first published in 1883. In this section I include historical fiction that uses the Robin Hood legend as its basis, in addition to a few important retellings of the legend. However, I do not include fantasy novels, like Nancy Springer's *Tales of Rowan Hood*, which are adventure romances that draw on the Middle Ages but are not set there. Nor do I include the vast library of retellings of the cycle of stories about Robin and his merry men.

321. Bull, Angela. *Robin Hood*. Illus. Nick Harris. DK Readers Series, Level 4. New York: DK Publishing, 2000. 48 pp. (0-789-45391-6 pb.) Elementary.

It will be hard for readers to understand whether Robin Hood is "Man or Myth" despite a chapter with that title; this is more of a storybook about Robin Hood that includes the familiar elements of Robin's struggle against the Sheriff of Nottingham. But the photos and other illustrations, as well as the introduction, make it seem like a biography. Glossary.

322. Cadnum, Michael. *Forbidden Forest: The Story of Little John and Robin Hood.* New York: Orchard, 2002. 218 pp. (0-439-31774-6 hc.) Junior-Senior.

Little John, a tanner's son, is 18 when he accidentally kills a man. The outlaw Red Roger rescues him, but Little John finds him too cruel and contemptuous of his fellow humans. Again he escapes, this time to Sherwood Forest, where he joins Robin Hood's band and helps 16-year-old Margaret, a merchant's daughter from Nottingham, when she is accused of murdering her new husband. Cadnum's portrayal of late medieval England is impressive, although his Sherwood is perhaps kinder than a real forest might be.

323. ———. *In a Dark Wood.* New York: Orchard, 1998. 246 pp. (0-531-30071-4 hc.) Senior.

Turning the Robin Hood story on its head, Cadnum makes the Sheriff of Nottingham his protagonist. Hardly one-sided and evil, the Sheriff is instead a thoughtful, troubled man. When he meets the famous outlaw, the two men learn mutual respect. All of the characters in this fine and careful presentation of late medieval England are adults, not teenagers, and Cadnum expertly draws on medieval art and literature (including *The Canterbury Tales*) for some of his portrayals of people and landscapes.

324. Furlong, Monica. *Robin's Country.* New York: Knopf, 1995. 139 pp. (0-679-89099-8 pb.) Middle.

In this very sweet forest romance with a vaguely medieval setting, a mute boy becomes a member of Robin Hood's band after escaping his cruel master. He proves his mettle by rescuing Robin, regains his voice, and discovers he is none other than the godson of King Richard Lionheart.

325. Granowsky, Alvin, et al. *Robin Hood / The Sheriff Speaks. A Classic Tale: Two Books in One.* Illus. David Griffin and Gregg Fitzhugh. Point of View Series. Austin, TX: Raintree / Steck-Vaughn, 1994. 48 pp. (0-811-42219-4 pb.) Middle.

Robin tells his story on one side of the book; flip to the other side and the Sheriff of Nottingham explains how he is trying to maintain order, but robbers like Robin Hood have no respect for the law.

326. Green, Roger Lancelyn. *The Adventures of Robin Hood.* Illus. Arthur Hall. 1956. London: Puffin, 1994. 294 pp. (0-14-036700-4 pb.) Middle.

Green uses medieval and early modern ballads as his sources for his retellings of the familiar tales, and he begins each story with a quotation from a ballad or a later source. This is an impressive, appealing version of the Robin Hood stories. Author's note.

327. Malcolmson, Anne. *The Song of Robin Hood.* Musical notation by Grace Castagnetta, illus. Virginia Lee Burton. 1947. Boston: Houghton Mifflin, 2000. 123 pp. (0-618-07186-5 hc.) Elementary.

Although the 15 original Robin Hood ballads set to music and accompanied by beautiful black and white pen and ink and scratchboard illustrations are meant for younger readers, anyone interested in the history of the Robin Hood story could benefit from this fine book. The preface explains the sources, and the illustrator explains her techniques in her own preface. The book ends with an extensive glossary. Caldecott Honor. Newbery Honor.

328. McKinley, Robin. *The Outlaws of Sherwood.* 1988. New York: Penguin/Firebird, 2002. 288 pp. (0-698-11959-2 pb.) Senior.

In her author's note, McKinley disavows any claim to be writing historical fiction, and her novel is more an adventure romance, with its heroic king and outlaws, than it is historical fiction. Yet it is also not fantasy, as it is sometimes called; rather, it is a retelling of the most familiar elements of the Robin Hood story in the form of a novel.

329. Serraillier, Ian. *Robin and his Merry Men: Ballads of Robin Hood.* Illus. Victor Ambrus. 1969. New York: Walck, 1970. 64 pp. Elementary.

In a companion to *Robin in the Greenwood,* Serraillier recasts more medieval and early modern ballads about Robin and people associated with him into verse.

330. ———. *Robin in the Greenwood: Ballads of Robin Hood.* Illus. Victor Ambrus. 1967. New York: Henry Z. Walck, 1968. 76 pp. Elementary.

Retelling medieval and early modern ballads in his own verses, Serraillier presents a narrative of the familiar Robin Hood story, from his birth and the gathering of his band of outlaws to his death at the hands of the cruel Prioress at Kirkley Hall. Nowhere in the text does he discuss his sources. Both black and white and color illustrations accompany the text.

331. Tomlinson, Theresa. *Child of the May*. New York: Orchard, 1998. 120 pp. (0-531-30118-4 hc.) Junior.
The book is set 15 years after *The Forestwife*, in a vaguely medieval Sherwood Forest, where Magda, the teenaged daughter of Little John, has been raised by Marian. Magda must accept her role as a healer, but she also has adventures when she chops off her hair, dresses as a boy, and accompanies the other outlaws on rescues and raids. Like its prequel, this is adventure-romance, not strictly historical fiction.

332. ———. *The Forestwife*. 1993. New York: Bantam Doubleday Dell, 1997. 170 pp. (0-440-41350-8 pb.) Junior.
An adventure-romance rather than a historical novel, the book portrays Robin Hood as a youth named Robert who has no patience for the suffering of peasants and women. It's up to Marian, a 15-year-old orphan who has escaped to the forest to avoid marriage to an odious old man, and the healer known as the Forestwife, to help Robert mature. Marian must also mature by accepting her role as the new Forestwife. Author's note.

333. Trease, Geoffrey. *Bows against the Barons*. Illus. C. Walter Hodges. 1934. Revised ed. New York: Meredith Press, 1966. 154 pp. Junior.
When the peasant boy Dickon kills one of the king's deer, he escapes to Sherwood Forest and is accepted into Robin Hood's band because of his archery skills. Soon he is involved in a plot by the peasantry to revolt against the rich barons. Although the book is an exciting adventure filled with many accurate historical details, Trease's incorporation of 20th-century political views about equality and social justice make it an anachronistic portrayal of class struggle.

CHAPTER EIGHT

Continental Europe, 1100–1500

War and plague seem to dominate the popular view of high and late medieval Europe, but much else was going on, as the books in this section make clear. St. Francis founded the Franciscan Order in 12th-century Italy, and he has been inspiring writers ever since. The feisty Queen Eleanor of Aquitaine, another 12th-century figure, has her own following among writers, as do the doomed lovers Heloise and Abelard. Troubadours, manuscript making, the rise of the universities, even the story of the Pied Piper of Hamelin are important during this era. In the 15th century, Gutenberg developed the technology of printing with moveable type, helping to bring about the end of the medieval period.

Nevertheless, war was a constant worry, both in Europe and in the far-off Holy Land. Because they are the subjects of so many books, the Crusades and Joan of Arc's role in the Hundred Years' War are dealt with in separate chapters, below.

Nonfiction

334. Boscielniak, Bruce, writer/illus. *Johann Gutenberg and the Amazing Printing Press.* Boston: Houghton Mifflin, 2003. 40 pp. (0-618-26351-9 hc.) Elementary.

Line drawings and watercolors illustrate this book, which is as much about the technology of printing as it is about Gutenberg. Moveable type was developed in China and Korea before it was in Europe, and Boscielniak explains the process, as well as Gutenberg's own innovations with inks and metal type.

335. Brooks, Polly Schoyer. *Queen Eleanor: Independent Spirit of the Medieval World.* Boston: Houghton Mifflin, 1983. 192 pp. (0-395-98139-5 pb.) Junior-Senior.
Readers will learn a great deal about medieval life from this beautifully written biography of Eleanor of Aquitaine (1122-1204), who was successively Queen of France and, after she divorced her first husband, Queen of England. Illustrations, chronology, further reading, index. ALA Notable Book, SLJ Best Book.

336. Bulla, Clyde Robert. *Song of St. Francis.* Illus. Valenti Angelo. New York: Thomas Crowell, 1952. 72 pp. (0-690-75223-7 lib. bdg.) Elementary.
In simple language and with simple two-color illustrations, Bulla and Angelo present Francis's biography, with an emphasis on his childhood. Bulla's music for his "Song of St. Francis" is printed on the endpapers.

337. Bunson, Margaret, and Matthew Bunson, writers/illus. *St. Francis of Assisi.* Saints You Should Know Series. Huntington, IN: Our Sunday Visitor, 1992. 56 pp. (0-87973-783-2 hc.) Elementary.
The foreword sets St. Francis against modern celebrities, who "seldom talk about the really important things." The saint's biography is written in workmanlike prose and the oil paintings on every page seem less than professional.

338. De Paola, Tomie, writer/illus. *Francis: The Poor Man of Assisi.* New York: Holiday House, 1982. 48 pp. (0-8234-0435-8 hc.) Elementary.
In his unmistakable style, here inspired by the art of Cimabue and Simone Martini in the Basilica of San Francesco in Assisi, de Paola tells the story of the late 12th-century to early 13th-century saint, from his birth to his death. He includes the stories of Clare and her sister Agnes becoming nuns, the Wolf of Gubbio, and St. Francis receiving the stigmata. Author's note, time line.

339. Fisher, Leonard Everett, writer/illus. *Gutenberg.* New York: Macmillan, 1993. 32 pp. (0-02-735238-2 hc.) Elementary.

Black and white acrylic paintings accompany this biography of the man who invented moveable metal type in the 1450s, helping move Europe from a manuscript age, where every single book had to be laboriously hand copied, to an information age, where many copies could be made in a single day. Because so little is known about Gutenberg's life, Fisher keeps his focus on the mechanics of printing and on Gutenberg's bad business sense, but the story he tells is still compelling. A Gutenberg Bible page is reproduced as the frontispiece.

340. Kaplan, Zoe Coralnik. *Eleanor of Aquitaine.* World Leaders of the Past and Present Series. New York: Chelsea House, 1987. 115 pp. (0-877-54522-7 lib. bdg.) Middle.

A biography of the woman who was married to both Louis VII of France and Henry II of England.

341. Lace, William W. *The Hundred Years' War.* World History Series. San Diego: Lucent Books, 1994. 112 pp. (1-56006-233-9 lib. bdg.) Junior-Senior.

Although the focus here is the political and military—not social— history of 14th- and 15th-century England and France, Lace spices his text with interesting vignettes and quotations from medieval sources. As in other books in the series, black and white maps, drawings, and re- productions of medieval and 19th-century art further complement the text. Chronology, further reading, bibliography, index.

342. Mayo, Margaret. *Brother Sun, Sister Moon: The Life and Stories of St. Francis.* Illus. Peter Malone. Boston: Little, Brown, 2000. 72 pp. (0-316-56466-4 lib. bdg.) Elementary.

Bright and charming paintings accompany this beautifully written, simple text, which introduces very young readers to the saint's biogra- phy, and then tells some of the stories associated with him.

343. Stewart, Gail B. *Life during the Spanish Inquisition.* The Way People Live Series. San Diego: Lucent Books, 1998. 96 pp. (1-56006-346-7 hc.) Junior-Senior.

From the beginnings of the Inquisition in early 13th-century France to its height in late 15th-century Spain, Stewart traces the causes and ef- fects of the courts of the Inquisitors. Readers will learn about the varieties of religions—Judaism, Islam, and Christian sects like the Cathari and the Albigensians, who were both considered heretics by the established

Catholic church. Those interested in medieval torture and execution will find plenty of information here. Although the Spanish Inquisition carried on through the 18th century, it is often associated with the Middle Ages. Notes, further reading, bibliography, index.

344. Wildsmith, Brian, writer/illus. *Saint Francis*. Grand Rapids, MI: Eerdmans, 1996. 36 pp. (0-8028-5123-1 hc.) Elementary.
In this large-format book St. Francis looks back on his own life from the distance of 800 years. He narrates his story in a simple, first-person text accompanied by bright, busy double-page illustrations that appealingly combine pen and ink with watercolors. Budding ornithologists will appreciate the varieties of birds on every page.

Fiction

345. Bosse, Malcolm. *Captives of Time*. New York: Bantam, 1987. 268 pp. (0-440-20311-2 pb.) Senior.
In the 14th-century, after 16-year-old Anne and her mute younger brother witness the brutal murder of their parents, they journey to their uncle's home, where he is constructing a clock. Plague and violent death make this a grim picture of the medieval world. BBYA.

346. Cunningham, Julia. *The Treasure Is the Rose*. Illus. Judy Graese. New York: Pantheon, 1973. 99 pp. (0-394-92674-9 lib. bdg.) Middle.
Somewhere in France in the year 1100, the young widow Ariane lives in poverty with her serving woman. Three ruffians take over her castle, having heard rumors of buried treasure. Ariane refuses to allow them to triumph despite their ill treatment of her, and they learn from her gentleness. Illustrated with pen and ink drawings, the book ends with the music and lyrics to "Ariane's Song" by Clyde Robert Bulla.

347. Dolan, Ellen M. *Oliver, the Page*. Illus. Marie Wabbes. Children of Other Times Series. St. Louis: McGraw-Hill, 1967. 25 pp. Elementary.
A boy is educated to be a knight.

348. Ellis, Deborah. *A Company of Fools*. Markham, Ontario, and Allston, Massachusetts: Fitzhenry and Whiteside, 2002. 191 pp. (1-55041-719-3 hc.) Middle-Junior.
In 1348, in a monastery outside Paris, young Henri is a friendless novice until the undisciplined Micah, an urban street boy, shows up. In

the face of the plague, the two choirboys join older monks in perform-ances meant to lift the spirits of Parisians. Then Micah is mistaken for a miracle worker and his celebrity leads to the downfall of the Com-pany of Fools. Author's note, maps, glossary.

349. French, Allen. *The Red Keep*. Illus. Andrew Wyeth. Bathgate, ND: Bethlehem Books, 1997. 384 pp. (1-883-93729-9 pb.) Middle-Junior.
In Burgundy in 1167, two robber barons try to take over a section of the country. They force Lady Anne d'Arcy out of her home, the Red Keep, and with the help of young Conan, she decides to regain her birthright.

350. Gregory, Kristiana. *Eleanor: Crown Jewel of Aquitaine*. The Royal Di-aries. New York: Scholastic, 2002. 200 pp. (0-439-16484-2 hc.) Middle.
A fictional diary of the years 1136–1137, when Eleanor became queen of France at age 15. Historical note, map, character list, and illustra-tions (many of them 19th-century representations of the Middle Ages) are appended.

351. Haugaard, Erik Christian. *Leif the Unlucky*. Boston: Houghton Mifflin, 1982. 206 pp. (0-395-32156-5 lib. bdg.) Junior.
A colony of Norse people settled Greenland in 986 and prospered for over 400 years—until 1410, when they were last heard from. Haugaard imagines their fate.

352. Henty, G. A. *At Agincourt: A Tale of the White Hoods of Paris*. Illus. Wal Paget. 1896. Mill Hall, PA: Preston Speed Publications, 2001. 323 pp. (1-887-15999-1 pb.) Middle-Junior.
A reprint of a 19th-century adventure story by an editor of *Boy's Own Magazine*. Here, as in his other novels, Henty sets a young man in the thick of historical events.

353. ———. *The Lion of St. Mark: A Tale of Venice in the 14th Century*. Illus. Gordon Browne. 1889. Mill Hall, PA: Preston Speed Publica-tions, 2000. 303 pp. (1-887-15953-3 pb.) Middle-Junior.
An adventure story of a young man living in Italy in 1380, when Venice and Genoa were at war.

354. Heuston, Kimberley. *Dante's Daughter*. Asheville, NC: Front Street, 2003. 312 pp. (1-886910-79-9 hc.) Junior-Senior.
In this fictional account of the life of Dante Alighieri's daughter, An-tonia is five when her father's political activities force the family to flee

Florence. She lives with the family of her uncle Duccio, the historical artist, and later journeys with her father to Paris. While he studies at the university, Antonia works at a stationer's shop in a *béguinage*, a community of lay sisters. Two years later, she returns to Duccio's house and becomes peripherally involved in the construction of his altarpiece, the *Maestà*. As years and troubles pass and Antonia's family's fortunes wane and then wax again, Antonia always finds herself in art, learning to fresco from Giotto as her father writes his *Purgatorio*. Heuston makes Antonia's improbable relationships with these artists believable by the deftness of her telling—she exaggerates neither the importance of Antonia's role in the art, nor the role of art in Antonia's rich and varied life. Complex characters, vivid details, and a sweeping narrative capture 14th-century Italian life.

355. Kelly, Eric. *The Trumpeter of Krakow*. 1928. New York: Simon and Schuster, 1966. 209 pp. (0-689-71571-4 pb.) Middle-Junior.

Using as a background the legend of the 13th-century trumpeter who stayed true to his oath, playing the hourly hymn to Mary even when the Tartars were attacking, Kelly tells the story of a 15th-century 15-year-old. Joseph's family escapes to Krakow from their Ukrainian estate when it is attacked. Joseph's father, the secret keeper of the mysterious Great Tarnov Crystal, finds a job as trumpeter, playing the same hymn to Mary, and he teaches it to Joseph. A confluence of events—alchemical explosions, attacks by Tartars, and a fire in the city—threatens Joseph's family as they try to guard the crystal and deliver it to the king. Although urban Poland comes alive in the descriptions, the plot relies heavily on coincidences. Newbery Medal.

356. Konigsburg, E. L., writer/illus. *A Proud Taste for Scarlet and Miniver*. New York: Atheneum, 1973. 202 pp. (0-689-30111-1 pb.) Middle-Junior.

Eleanor of Aquitaine waits in heaven for her husband Henry II, who is still in Purgatory. Waiting with her in heaven are Abbot Suger, Henry's mother, the Empress Matilda, and the famous knight, William Marshal. They each tell their own version of the life of Eleanor and Henry in 12th-century France and England.

357. Laird, Christa. *The Forgotten Son*. New York: Walker, 1990. 192 pp. (0-862-03477-9 hc.) Junior.

The famous 12th-century lovers Heloise and Abelard had a son. In this novel, Laird tells his story; he is brought up by his aunt while his parents—whom he longs to know—live the monastic life.

358. Napoli, Donna Jo. *Breath*. New York: Atheneum, 2003. 272 pp. (0-689-86174-5 hc.) Senior.

In Hameln, Germany, in 1284, 12-year-old Salz has survived cystic fibrosis longer than most medieval children would because of his grandmother's remedies. His farmer father and brothers, however, have little use for him, and the villagers regard him with suspicion. Then the rains come, followed by rats, and then by a mysterious disease. Salz and his grandmother and her coven try pagan remedies, to no avail, and the church can't help, either. When a piper is able to lure the rats out of town, the disease still lingers; unbeknownst to the villagers, it is caused by ergot poisoning in the grain, which has the same chemical properties as LSD. Napoli combines the Pied Piper story with theories about medieval ergot poisoning in her rich, layered tale, but the story belongs to Salz, who is always suspect because he is different.

359. O'Dell, Scott. *The Road to Damietta*. 1985. New York: Ballantine Books, 1987. 228 pp. (0-449-70233-2 pb.) Junior-Senior.

The life of St. Francis of Assisi is illuminated through the eyes of 13-year-old Ricca, who has a crush on him. The daughter of a wealthy merchant in 13th-century Italy, Ricca follows Francis to Egypt during the Fifth Crusade; unconvincingly, she not only speaks fluent Arabic but views Muslims from a 20th-century perspective. This is far from being O'Dell's most successful novel.

360. Olofsson, Helena, writer/illus. *The Little Jester*. Trans. from Swedish by Helena Board. New York: R & S Books, 2002. 28 pp. (9-129-65499-8 hc.) Elementary.

When a group of French monks feeds a hungry little boy dressed as a jester, he thanks them by performing his music and tricks in front of a painting of a weeping Madonna. This leads to the abbot becoming angry—and a bit of a miracle.

361. Pernoud, Regine. *A Day with a Troubadour*. Illus. Giorgio Bacchin. Trans. Dominique Clift. Minneapolis: Runestone Press, 1997. 48 pp. (0-822-51915-1 lib. bdg.) Middle.
Factual information about troubadours is combined with the story of Peire Vidal, a fictional troubadour in 12th-century Provence.

362. Pyle, Howard, writer/illus. *Otto of the Silver Hand*. 1888. New York: Dover, 1967. 173 pp. (0-486-21784-1 pb.) Middle.
In Germany in the high Middle Ages, motherless Otto is brought up by the kindly monks in a monastery, but he must return to his father's castle at a dangerous time: his family is involved in a feud with a neighboring family, and Otto becomes a pawn.

363. Robertson, Bruce. *Marguerite Makes a Book*. Illus. Kathryn Hewitt. Los Angeles: Getty, 1999. 44 pp. (0-89236-372-X hc.) Elementary.
In 14th-century Paris, young Marguerite helps her frail father finish a book of hours commissioned by a noblewoman. Lavish, delightful, and accurate paintings illustrate how manuscripts were made. Glossary.

364. Sauerwein, Leigh. *Song for Eloise*. Asheville, NC: Front Street, 2003. 136 pp. (1-886910-90-1 hc.) Middle.
In late 12th-century France, 15-year-old Eloise is married to a much older man. Meanwhile, her childhood friend Thomas travels throughout the land as a troubadour, accompanied by a juggler. In the end, Eloise and Thomas are reunited.

365. Skurzynski, Gloria. *Manwolf*. New York: Clarion, 1981. 177 pp. (0-395-30079-7 hc.) Junior.
In late 14th-century Poland, Adam—whose mother Danusha is a serf on a nobleman's manor, and whose father (whom he has never met) is a nobleman—grows up with a condition that makes him look wolf-like, with red teeth and skin and excessive facial hair. The novel begins when 16-year-old Danusha is required to serve a passing nobleman, who rapes her. Count Reinmar suffers from the same disease Adam inherits. As Adam becomes an object of fear and derision to the serfs on the manor, Danusha must escape to the forest to save him. Yet when he is captured and accused of being a werewolf, Adam finds friends in unexpected places. Skurzynski treats historical details respectfully in this complex, thought-provoking work. Author's note. BBYA.

366. ———. *The Minstrel in the Tower.* Illus. Julek Heller. New York: Random House, 1988. 64 pp. (0-394-99598-8 lib. bdg.) Elementary.
In France at the end of the 12th century, with their mother ill and their father never returned from the Crusades, 11-year-old Roger and his 8-year-old sister Alice must take a three-day journey to Bordeaux to find their uncle. Along the way, they are captured by serfs who hope to earn a ransom from them. Alice's tree-climbing skills and Roger's musicianship help save them.

367. ———. *Spider's Voice.* New York: Atheneum, 1999. 220 pp. (0-689-82149-2 hc.) Middle-Junior.
In 12th-century France, the mute boy Aran becomes a go-between for Heloise and Peter Abelard after Abelard rescues him. Readers learn about the ferment of learning at the University of Paris during the period known as the Twelfth-Century Renaissance, and they are privy to the forbidden love affair between Heloise and Abelard, as well as the lovers' later entry into religious institutions. Author's note.

368. ———. *What Happened in Hamelin.* 1979. New York: Random House, 1993. 192 pp. (0-679-83645-4 pb.) Middle-Junior.
In the German town of Hamelin in the year 1284, a plague of rats appears. The 13-year-old baker's apprentice, Geist, befriends the mysterious stranger who shows up one day offering to help the town with its rat problem. But the stranger becomes more sinister as the days pass, and in the end, he leads the children away from the town, to which they never return. Skurzynski uses historical records to tell the tale of the Pied Piper in this compelling, thoughtful novel. Author's note. Christopher Award, Horn Book Honor List.

369. Welch, Ronald [Ronald Oliver Felton]. *Bowman of Crecy.* Illus. Ian Ribbons. 1966. Oxford: Oxford University Press, 1997. 186 pp. (0-192-71746-4 pb.) Middle-Junior.
For those who love descriptions of battles and weapons, this novel about Hugh Fletcher and his group of forest outlaws, who serve King Edward III fighting against the French at Crécy, will appeal.

CHAPTER NINE

The Crusades

For complex reasons that had as much to do with politics, economics, weather, and food supplies as they did with religion, the Crusades began in 1095. For the next two hundred years, European Christians voyaged to the Holy Land to try to reclaim Jerusalem from Muslims. Some of the crusades to the Holy Land involved kings and knights; others, such as the Peasants' Crusade, involved ordinary people. In the 13th century, thousands of commoners took part in what has been called the Children's Crusade, although information about it is confusing and contradictory—and based on two separate events. However, historians now conclude that while some children may have been involved, the majority of the participants were adult peasants, and none of them made it to Jerusalem.

For some members of the upper classes, on the other hand, Outremer became a second home and crusading became a career. The Christian Kingdom of Jerusalem, in what is now Israel and parts of Syria, was established in the 11th century. Its king was a French aristocrat. In the 12th century, Eleanor of Aquitaine accompanied her husband Louis VII of France on the Second Crusade. The Crusades ended in 1291, when the port city of Acre fell to the Arabs.

The religious conflicts, the adventure of the difficult journey to an exotic place, and the colorful images of knights and battles have sparked the imaginations of many writers. Recently, Saladin, the 12th-century Muslim leader who fought against the English king Richard the Lionhearted, has also attracted authorial attention; works about him and other Muslims appear in chapter 11, "Beyond Western Europe."

Nonfiction

370. Biel, Timothy L. *The Crusades*. World History Series. San Diego: Lucent Books, 1995. 128 pp. (1-56006-245-2 lib. bdg.) Junior-Senior.
Biel sets the Crusades within the social context of medieval Europe, explaining feudalism, the lives of peasants and nobles, and the role of the church. Then he shifts to the Crusades themselves: the politics, economics, and military history. Inset quotations from medieval sources enliven the text. Many of the black and white illustrations are taken from 19th-century sources, which give a romantic view of events. Maps, chronology, glossary, bibliography, index.

371. Child, John, Nigel Kelly, and Martyn Whittock. *The Crusades*. New York: Peter Bedrick Books, 1994. 64 pp. (0-87226-119-0 lib. bdg.) Middle.
Color photos of existing buildings, maps, and medieval art, along with inset quotations from medieval and modern sources and minibiographies of important figures, accompany the text, which introduces readers to Islamic culture and beliefs, the conflict over Jerusalem, medieval Europe—and finally, the various Crusades themselves. Instead of oversimplifying, the text shows how complex the situation was, and it gives a balanced view of the groups involved. Index.

372. Chrisp, Peter. *The Crusades*. Themes in History. East Sussex, England: Wayland, 1992. 48 pp. (0-7502-0475-3 lib. bdg.) Elementary-Middle.
An impressive collection of photos of medieval art from both Eastern and Western Europe and the Middle East illustrates this fair-minded, well-written volume. Quotations from medieval writers appear in inset boxes; one box juxtaposes two accounts of the same event, one written by a Muslim historian, the other by a Christian priest. The author asks readers to look for the words that show the different attitudes between

the two writers. The last chapter discusses the legacy of the Crusades in later centuries. Time line, glossary, further reading, index.

373. Kerhaghan, Pamela. *The Crusades: Cultures in Conflict*. Cambridge: Cambridge University Press, 1993. 64 pp. (0-521-44617-1 pb.) Middle.
This history of the Crusades gives both Eastern and Western perspectives and looks at the different Crusades, the victims of the Crusades, and the Crusades' legacy. The book includes questions and activities.

374. Nicolle, David. *The Crusades*. Illus. Richard Hood. Oxford: Osprey Publishing, 1988. 64 pp. (0-850-45854-4 pb.) Middle-Junior-Senior.
This book is actually an authoritative military history written for adults; the color plates and short text will appeal to readers with a special interest in the military aspects of the Crusades.

375. Rice, Earle, Jr. *Life during the Crusades*. The Way People Live Series. San Diego: Lucent, 1998. 96 pp. (1-56006-379-3 hc.) Junior-Senior.
Although this book is admirable in its goal of representing both "the Christian West and the Muslim East," its reliance on outdated sources and its attempt to cover too much material make it less reliable than it could have been. The Crusades are a complex subject and Rice gives a historical overview before he treats topics like feudalism and the details of daily life in Christian and Muslim areas. Rice's selection of information is sometimes unbalanced. For example, the Muslim world is portrayed as male-dominated but Rice does not note that the Christian world was equally patriarchal; towns in Muslim areas are portrayed as cramped and dirty, but there is no mention of cramped, dirty Christian towns. Yet there is still much valuable information in the book.

376. Steffens, Bradley. *The Children's Crusade*. World Disasters Series. San Diego: Lucent Books, 1991. 64 pp. (1-560-06019-0 hc.) Middle.
Steffens provides the cultural context for the Children's Crusade, including information about medieval pilgrimages and religious beliefs. The end of the book skips forward to the Israeli Six-Day War of 1967 and the 1991 Gulf War, but Steffens doesn't make a clear enough connection between these conflicts and the Children's Crusade to warrant their inclusion. Index.

377. Suskind, Richard. *Cross and Crescent: The Story of the Crusades*. Illus. Victor Lazzaro. New York: W. W. Norton, 1967. 84 pp. Middle-Junior.

Illustrated with black and white drawings, this text covers the social conditions in Europe at the time of the Crusades. It briefly introduces readers to Islam, and seems to imply that Muslims may have brought the Crusades on themselves by their actions. The portrayal of Christians is more balanced, although Richard the Lionhearted's massacre of unarmed prisoners goes unmentioned, and Suskind celebrates the image of the brave Crusader knight. As he explains the successive crusades, he informs readers about related topics: Constantinople, armor and weapons, assassins, the Knights Templar, etc. Index.

378. Unstead, R. J. *Living in a Crusader Land*. Illus. Victor Ambrus. Reading, MA: Addison-Wesley, 1971. 44 pp. (0-201-08497-X hc.) Elementary.

First published in Great Britain, this very readable book begins with a definition of the Crusades, an explanation of why they took place, and a discussion of the leaders, before settling into the topic of fighting and living in Outremer. Unstead demonstrates the dependence Christian knights who settled in the Crusader states had on Muslim servants and city officials, and the intermingling of cultures. Despite the brevity of the text and its elementary school audience, the book is a fine introduction to a subject few Americans of any age know much about. Index.

379. Williams, Jay. *Knights of the Crusades*. A Horizon Caravel Book. New York: American Heritage Publishing, 1962. 155 pp. Junior.

The book begins with a chapter about the Norman Conquest and William the Conqueror's knights before focusing on the political and military history of the Crusades themselves. The chief appeal of this book is its excellent color reproductions of medieval art, including some Islamic manuscript illuminations.

Fiction

380. Beckman, Thea. *Crusade in Jeans*. 1973. Translated from the Dutch *Kruistocht in spijkerbroek*. Asheville, NC: Front Street, 2003. 313 pp. (1-886910-26-X pp.) Junior-Senior.

Almost-15-year-old Dolf time-travels to 13th-century Germany, where he finds himself trapped in the midst of the Children's Crusade. Appalled by the condition of the children, he becomes a leader, helping to organize, feed, and protect them on their march from Germany to Brindisi, on the heel of Italy. Never revealing his origins to his companions, Dolf learns a great deal about medieval travel, attitudes, and especially Christianity. Golden Pen Award (annual Dutch award for the best book for young people).

381. Bradford, Karleen. *There Will Be Wolves*. New York: Dutton, 1992. 195 pp. (0-525-67539-6 pb.) Junior.

In Cologne in 1096, 16-year-old Ursula, the daughter of an apothecary, is condemned as a witch, partly because of her love of books, reading, and healing. She is sent on the People's Crusade to Jerusalem. Although the novel tells an exciting story informed by research about the People's Crusade, Ursula's attitudes—and those of the other good characters in the book—are modern, not medieval, while evil characters are often characterized by their acceptance of ideas common to medieval culture, particularly religious intolerance.

382. Cadnum, Michael. *The Book of the Lion*. New York: Viking, 2000. 204 pp. (0-670-88386-7 hc.) Junior-Senior.

In the 12th century, 17-year-old Edmund becomes a squire and travels to the Holy Land to fight in the Crusades. Most of this splendid evocation of the medieval milieu—its brutality along with its sweetness—is spent on the journey. Edmund's attitudes, including his opinions about religion and women, reflect those of a 12th-century youth, not a modern one. Author's note. National Book Award finalist.

383. ———. *The Dragon Throne*. Forthcoming.

The third book in the sequence that began with *The Book of the Lion* features both Eleanor of Aquitaine and Prince John, among others.

384. ———. *The Leopard Sword*. New York: Viking, 2002. 208 pp. (0-670-89908-9 hc.) Junior-Senior.

In this sequel to *The Book of the Lion*, told from Edmund's friend Hubert's point of view, the squires and knights journey home from the Crusades. On the way Hubert faces fights with both infidels and fellow Christians, shipwreck near Rome, love, and the ties of loyalty to his friend.

[Crossley-Holland, Kevin. Arthur Trilogy: Book 2, *At the Crossing Places*, and Book 3, *King of the Middle March*. *See* Arthurian Legend, chapter 13.]

385. Henty, G. A. *A Knight of the White Cross: A Tale of the Siege of Rhodes*. Illus. Ralph Peacock. 1895. Mill Hall, PA: Preston Speed Publications, 1999. 408 pp. (1-887-15925-8 pb.) Middle-Junior.
Young Gervaise Tresham goes to the Holy Land to join the Knights Hospitallers during the 15th century. He becomes a captain of a war galley and fights during the Siege of Rhodes.

386. ———. *Winning His Spurs: A Story of the Crusades*. 1882. Mill Hall, PA: Preston Speed Publications, 2000. 324 pp. (1-887-15934-7 pb.) Middle-Junior.
In the 12th century, young Cuthbert de Lance leaves England to go to the Third Crusade as a page, and ends up helping King Richard.

387. Hewes, Agnes Danforth. *A Boy of the Lost Crusade*. Illus. Gustaf Tenggren. Boston: Houghton-Mifflin, 1923. 279 pp. Junior.
Roland Arnot is a French boy whose father has been gone to the Crusades for two years when a strange monk shows up calling the children to undertake a crusade themselves. His mother dresses as a boy and accompanies Roland, but she soon dies and Roland joins a group of Crusader monks, thus making it to Palestine. He learns Arabic from Samson, a kind Syrian shepherd, helps the Crusaders, and finally finds his father. This old-fashioned novel, illustrated with color plates and maps, romanticizes the Crusades. Hewes also wrote *The Sword of Roland Arnot*.

388. Jewett, Eleanore Myers. *Big John's Secret*. Illus. Frederick T. Chapman. New York: Viking, 1962. 236 pp. Junior.
In the 13th century, during the reign of King John, an English boy's search for his father takes him to the Crusades and to the Sultan's court, where he accompanies St. Francis of Assisi.

389. Jinks, Catherine. *Pagan in Exile*. Cambridge, MA: Candlewick, 2004. (0-7636-2020-3 hc.) Junior-Senior.
The second book in the Pagan Chronicles directly follows the first, Pagan's Crusade. In 1188 Pagan accompanies Lord Roland to France, where they find Roland's family involved in a feud with their neighbors.

390. ———. *Pagan's Crusade*. Illus. Peter Seve. Cambridge, MA: Candlewick Press, 2003. 256 pp. (0-763-62019-X lib. bdg.) Junior-Senior.

In 1187, 16-year-old Pagan, who lives on the streets of Jerusalem, becomes the squire of Lord Roland, a Templar knight who is so perfect he seems like St. George's brother. Then Saladin takes Jaffa and other Crusader cities, and Jerusalem is next on his list. It falls to Lord Roland to command the Templar knights, and to Pagan to keep Roland from sacrificing himself. Behind Pagan's sarcastic voice is a sensitive, intelligent youth who has finally found a father figure. First published in Australia, this is the first of the four Pagan Chronicles by Australian author Jinks.

391. ———. *Pagan's Scribe*. Cambridge, MA: Candlewick, 2005. (0-7636-2022-X hc.) Junior-Senior.

The last volume in the Pagan Chronicles takes place several years after the third. Pagan has become an archbishop and Isidore, his young scribe, narrates the story.

392. ———. *Pagan's Vows*. Cambridge, MA: Candlewick, 2004. (0-7636-2021-1 hc.) Junior-Senior.

The third book in the Pagan Chronicles won the Children's Book Council of Australia Book of the Year for Older Readers. In it, Pagan and Roland become novices in a monastery.

393. Treece, Henry. *The Children's Crusade*. Illus. Christine Price. London: Bodley Head, 1958. 246 pp. Junior.

According to legends, in the year 1212 a 12-year-old shepherd boy led the ill-fated Children's Crusade to save Jerusalem from the infidels. Treece tells the story of Geoffrey and Alys de Villacours, two children of the French nobility who followed the peasant boy. They are separated, made slaves, and eventually find their way home again.

394. Welch, Ronald [Ronald Oliver Felton]. *Knight Crusader*. 1954. New York: Oxford University Press, 1979. 246pp. Junior-Senior.

Seventeen-year-old Philip d'Aubigny, the son of a Norman Crusader knight, has lived in Outremer, the Christian Kingdom of Jerusalem, all his life. Philip serves in the house of a Turkish nobleman, is kidnapped by assassins, and fights with Richard I. In the culturally diverse world of the novel, which is set around 1185, women are scarcely seen, but the variety of religions—as well as attitude toward them—is admirably portrayed. However, Welch's Anglophilia is evident in the way he paints both King Richard and the English soldiery. Carnegie Medal.

CHAPTER TEN

Joan of Arc

The 15th-century French peasant who heard voices telling her to help her country by going to war is a favorite for writers of fiction and non-fiction, picture books and novels—and why not? As a teenager she was able to convince important and powerful men to take her seriously. She first heard Saints Margaret, Catherine, and Michael speaking to her when she was 12, and a few years later, she found herself leading the French troops as they came to the aid of the besieged city of Orléans in 1429, during the Hundred Years' War. Her greatest triumph came when she stood beside Charles VII as he was crowned King of France. Yet when she was captured by the Burgundians, who were allies of the English, the French king didn't ransom her. Sold to the English, she was tried for witchcraft and heresy—one of the charges against her was that she wore men's clothing. Finally, in 1431, Joan was burned at the stake.

The records of Joan's trial—as well as those of her trial of rehabilitation, which took place 25 years after her death—survive, giving us a wealth of information about her. In the second trial, her childhood neighbors, her family, and her friends testified about Joan, revealing fascinating details of French peasant life. In the end, the charges against her were dropped, and almost five hundred years later, in 1920, she was named a saint.

Nonfiction

395. Banfield, Susan. *Joan of Arc*. World Leaders Past and Present. New York: Chelsea House, 1988. 112 pp. (0-87754-556-1 lib. bdg.) Middle-Junior.

In order to illustrate Joan's appeal, Banfield begins with a fictional vignette of a soldier who, at hope's end, is inspired by Joan to fight on. Then she sets the political scene in France before turning to Joan's biography, which takes up most of the rest of the book. Black and white photos and reproductions of art from various centuries (only some of it identified) appear on every page. Further reading, chronology, index.

396. Boutet de Monvel, Maurice, writer/illus. *Joan of Arc*. Intro. by Gerald Gottlieb. New York: Viking, 1980. 56 pp. (0-670-40735-6 hc.) Elementary.

A translation and reprint of an 1896 French biography, from the copy in the Pierpont Morgan Library. Although Boutet de Monvel's text has historical flaws in it, his charming color illustrations, which may have been inspired by both Japanese prints and medieval manuscripts, greatly influenced later children's book illustration.

397. Brooks, Polly Schoyer. *Beyond the Myth: The Story of Joan of Arc*. Boston: Houghton Mifflin, 1999. 178 pp. (0-395-98138-7 pp.) Junior-Senior.

This clear-eyed, clearly written biography begins by setting the political scene in 15th-century France that led to civil war and the English incursions, before turning to Joan herself: her life, her accomplishments, her death, and the trial of rehabilitation that cleared her of charges of heresy. Well-chosen black and white photos and drawings complement the impressive text, which makes accessible without ever oversimplifying the complex political maneuverings of Joan's time. Author's note, bibliography, index. BBYA.

398. Bull, Angela. *Joan of Arc*. DK Readers Series, Level 4. New York: DK Publishing, 2000. 48 pp. (0-789-45719-9 hc.) Elementary.

Joan's biography is written like fiction; Bull tells us what Joan thinks and feels. Color photos and illustrations, along with sidebars on every page, give some of the background of medieval life. In one sidebar, Bull tells readers that some people believe Joan's voices were sent by God, while others think they were hallucinations brought about by anorexia.

399. Christopher, Tracy. *Joan of Arc: Soldier Saint.* Junior World Biography Series. New York: Chelsea House, 1993. 76 pp. (0-791-01767-2 lib. bdg.) Middle.
A biography of the saint.

400. Corey, Shana. *Joan of Arc.* Illus. Dan Andreasen. Step into Reading Series. New York: Random House, 2003. 48 pp. (0-375-90620-7 lib. bdg.) Elementary.
Line-and-wash illustrations accompany this picture-book biography that focuses on Joan's heroism.

401. Fisher, Aileen. *Jeanne D'Arc.* Illus. Ati Forberg. New York: Crowell, 1970. 52 pp. Elementary.
Gorgeous pencil sketches and color illustrations complement this simply but elegantly told biography of Joan's life from age 11, when raiders attacked her village, to her death.

402. Hodges, Margaret. *Joan of Arc: The Lily Maid.* Illus. Robert Rayevsky. New York: Holiday House, 1999. 32 pp. (0-823-41424-8 hc.) Elementary.
In simple language, Joan's story from her peasant youth to her death is told and illustrated with charming etchings and drypoint prints. The text ends with a historical note.

403. Lace, William W. *Joan of Arc and the Hundred Years' War.* In World History Series. Berkeley Heights, NJ: Enslow, 2003. 128 pp. (0-766-01938-1 lib. bdg.) Middle-Junior.
A biography of the 15th-century peasant girl who was eventually burned at the stake.

404. Poole, Josephine. *Joan of Arc.* Illus. Angela Barrett. New York: Random House, 1999. 32 pp. (0-099-55361-9 pb.) Elementary.
Illustrated with striking paintings, this biography focuses less on political events than on Joan's spirituality. She is shown being visited by angels in prison, for example. Instead of telling the details of Joan's death, Poole writes, "A saint is like a star. A star and a saint shine forever." Time line, map.

405. Stanley, Diane, writer/illus. *Joan of Arc*. New York: Morrow Junior
   Books, 1998. 48 pp. (0-688-14330-X lib. bdg.) Elementary.
Beginning with an explanation of the Hundred Years' War—including
what life would have been like for children who had never known
peace—Stanley tells the story of Joan from her childhood to her death.
A sumptuous painting appears on every other page, and Stanley sticks
to the historical record in her impressive biography. Pronunciation
guide, bibliography.

406. Storr, Catherine. *Joan of Arc*. Illus. Robert Taylor. Milwaukee:
   Raintree Steck-Vaughn, 1987. 32 pp. (0-817-22111-5 lib. bdg.) Elementary.
Based on Marina Warner's *Joan of Arc* (London, 1981), the text tells
the story simply, from Joan's visions to her death. Like the text, the
paintings are generally accurate, if unremarkable.

407. Tompert, Ann. *Joan of Arc: Heroine of France*. Illus. Michael Gar-
   land. Honesdale, PA: Boyds Mills, 2003. 32 pp. (1-59078-009-4 hc.)
   Elementary.
An easy-to-read biography that does a nice job of presenting the historical events, illustrated by vivid pictures. Index.

Fiction

408. Dana, Barbara. *Young Joan*. New York: HarperCollins, 1991. 340
   pp. (0-06-440661-X pb.) Middle.
Joan, in prison at age 19, tells the story of her childhood up until the
time she leaves home. Speaking from a first-person viewpoint in a
stilted, pseudo-medieval style, Joan is cloyingly sweet. The story stays
close to the historical account of Joan's childhood.

409. Garden, Nancy. *Dove and Sword: A Novel of Joan of Arc*. New
   York: Farrar, Straus & Giroux, 1995. 237 pp. (0-374-34476-0 hc.)
   Junior-Senior.
Gabrielle, a peasant from Joan's village, accompanies Joan on some of
her wartime travels. Gabrielle falls in love with a nobleman's son. Al-
ready an accomplished healer, she learns more about medicine by

dressing as a boy and becoming apprentice to the army's surgeon. Author's note.

410. Goodwin, Marie D. *Where the Towers Pierce the Sky*. New York: Four Winds Press, 1989. 185 pp. (0-02-736871-8 hc.) Junior.
Thirteen-year-old Lizzie, a 20th-century American teenager, time-travels to 1429 France with Jacques, an apprentice astrologer. She learns medieval French, as well as about repellent medieval attitudes, like anti-Semitism. Joan of Arc is a minor character; the book is more concerned with Lizzie's adventures in the 15th century.

CHAPTER ELEVEN

Beyond Western Europe

For many years the word *medieval* applied only to events that happened between 500 and 1500 in Western Europe. However, that has changed recently as people have begun to see a broader perspective of the world and to compare contemporaneous events in different parts of the globe. The books in this chapter cover two important cultures that coexisted with—and often influenced—Western Europe: Byzantium and the Islamic world. A third area, Asia, is dealt with obliquely; although Marco Polo was Italian, he is included in this section because so much that has been written about him focuses on his travels to China. However, I make no attempt to include books about all parts of the world between 500–1500; that task would require another bibliography altogether. Here, I keep the focus on cultures that came into contact with Western Europe in the medieval period.

Nonfiction

411. Bandon, Alex. *The Travels of Marco Polo*. Illus. Patrick O'Brien. Austin, TX: Raintree / Steck-Vaughn, 2000. 48 pp. (0-7398-1485-0 lib. bdg.) Elementary.
Bandon tells about the 13th-century traveler's life and his journeys to Asia. Paintings and maps are included. Time line, glossary, index.

412. Corrick, James. *The Byzantine Empire.* World History Series. San Diego: Lucent Books, 1997. 112 pp. (1-56006-307-6 lib. bdg.) Junior-Senior.

Illustrated with black and white paintings, photos, and drawings, as well as with quotations from ancient, medieval, and modern sources, the book introduces readers to the history and culture of the Byzantine Empire. Social classes, Byzantine Christianity, literature, and art are briefly discussed, but the focus is on political history. Time line, further reading, bibliography, index.

413. Greene, Carol. *Marco Polo: Voyager to the Orient.* People of Distinction Biographies. Chicago: Children's Press, 1987. 109 pp. (0-516-03229-1 lib. bdg.) Middle.

Sprinkled with quotations from *The Travels of Marco Polo*, this workmanlike biography informs readers about Marco Polo's life and travels, sometimes suggesting what the young Venetian might have thought and felt about the things he saw in Asia. Some negative stereotypes about life in medieval Venice make their way into the text. Black and white illustrations are included. Map, chronology, index.

414. Herbert, Janis. *Marco Polo for Kids: His Marvelous Journey to China; 21 Activities.* Chicago: Chicago Review Press, 2001. 144 pp. (1-55652-377-7 pb.) Middle.

The story of Marco Polo's journey to China is interspersed with information about the political and cultural history of Turkey, the Mongol Empire, and Persia; Christianity, Islam, and Zoroastrianism; Genghis Khan and Kublai Khan, etc.—too much for one book. The activities range from learning Turkish words to staging an opera.

415. Kent, Zachary. *Marco Polo.* The World's Great Explorers Series. Chicago: Children's Press, 1992. 128 pp. (0-516-03070-1 lib. bdg.) Middle.

Using quotations from *The Travels of Marco Polo* within his own text, Kent tells the story of the Venetian explorer's life and travels. Appealing color photos and artwork enhance the story, but their sources are rarely identified—is this a medieval European portrait of Kublai Khan? Is this a modern picture of Chinese miners? Map, chronology, glossary, further reading, index.

416. Macdonald, Fiona. *Marco Polo: A Journey through China.* Illus. Mark Bergin. New York: Franklin Watts, 1998. 32 pp. (0-531-14453-4 lib. bdg.) Elementary-Middle.

Instead of offering a biography of the explorer, this volume focuses on the time in which Marco Polo lived, his journey, and the cultures of the places he visited. Double-page spreads with detailed color illustrations show different parts of his trip, and inset paragraphs provide more information.

417. Rumford, James. *Traveling Man: The Journey of Ibn Battuta, 1325–1354.* Boston: Houghton Mifflin, 2001. 40 pp. (0-618-08366-9 hc.) Elementary.

In 1325, the Moroccan Muslim Ibn Battuta started a 22-year journey from Morocco to China and further that began as a pilgrimage to Mecca. He wrote a book about his travels that Rumford uses as the basis of this gorgeously illustrated picture book—which could also be of interest to older readers who want to know about the history of Islam.

418. Stanley, Diane, writer/illus. *Saladin: Noble Prince of Islam.* New York: HarperCollins, 2002. 48 pp. (0-688-17136-2 lib. bdg.) Middle.

A biography of the 12th-century Muslim leader who defended his homeland against Christians, including Richard the Lionhearted, during the Third Crusade. Some of Stanley's gorgeous paintings and decorations, which adorn every other page, are inspired by Persian miniature paintings. Author's note, glossary, bibliography.

419. Taylor, Robert. *Life in Genghis Khan's Mongolia.* The Way People Live Series. San Diego: Lucent Books, 2001. 96 pp. (1-56006-348-3 lib. bdg.) Junior-Senior.

Genghis Khan lived from around 1162–1227 and ruled a huge empire that stretched from Poland to the China Sea, and from the Persian Gulf to the Arctic. Using photos of modern Mongolian nomads, as well as other black and white illustrations, Taylor discusses nomadic life, tribal culture, and religious life as well as Genghis Khan's political life and wars. Bibliography, further reading, index.

420. Townson, Duncan. *Muslim Spain.* Cambridge Topic Books. Cambridge: Cambridge University Press, 1973. 48 pp. (0-521-20251-5 pb.) Junior-Senior.

Starting with an account of Muhammad's life and the expansion of Islam, the book then turns to the history of Visigothic Spain and the coming of Islam to Spain. Townson describes tenth-century Cordoba, with its libraries, gardens, impressive architecture and decorative arts, its crafts and trades, its mingling of Arabs and Berbers, Christians and Jews. Other chapters focus on Islam as a religion, the mosque, and Muslim learning. The last chapter deals with the end of Muslim Spain in the 13th century. The glossary includes a list of English words that come from Arabic.

421. Twist, Clint. *Marco Polo: Overland to Medieval China.* Beyond the Horizons Series. Austin, TX: Raintree Steck-Vaughn, 1994. 46 pp. (0-8114-7251-5 lib. bdg.) Elementary.

Marco Polo left Venice in 1271 at the age of 17 and returned from Asia 20 years later. Twist sets the stage for his travels, briefly describing the political and cultural situation in 13th-century Venice and Europe, the friction between East and West, the various religions, the modes of travel in both Europe and Asia, the making of paper and silk, and the kinds of things Marco Polo would have seen on his travels. Bright photos, medieval art, maps, and inset paragraphs accompany these comparisons between medieval Europe and Asia and make this an appealing book. Glossary, further reading, index.

Fiction

422. Barrett, Tracy. *Anna of Byzantium.* New York: Dell Laurel Leaf, 1999. 211 pp. (0-440-41536-5 pb.) Junior.

This novel is based on the life of Anna Comnena (1083–1153), who was to become empress of the Byzantine Empire until she was supplanted by her younger brother and scheming grandmother. From the convent to which she has been banished, Anna looks back on her childhood in the imperial palace in Constantinople (modern-day Istanbul): her studies, the court intrigues, and the conflict between her mother and her grandmother. Readers will become aware of some of the differences between Western Europe and Byzantium, including the power accorded to Byzantine royal women. Anna is the author of *The Alexiad,* an epic poem about her father's life. Author's note. BBYA.

423. Heide, Florence Parry, and Judith Heide Gilliland. *The House of Wisdom*. Illus. Mary GrandPré. New York: DK Ink, 1999. 48 pp. (0-789-42562-9 hc.) Elementary.

In ninth-century Baghdad, Ishaq's father is a scholar in the service of the historical figure Caliph al-Ma'mun, who built the great library the House of Wisdom. Although Ishaq grows up surrounded by manuscripts and learning, he doesn't understand their significance until he travels to distant lands in search of more manuscripts for the caliph. The lush, full-color illustrations are inspired by the decorative patterns in Islamic art.

424. Temple, Frances. *The Beduin's Gazelle*. New York: Orchard, 1996. 150 pp. (0-531-09519-3 hc.) Middle-Junior.

In 1302, Etienne, the French scholar from Temple's *The Ramsay Scallop*, makes it to the city of Fez, where he meets Atiyah, a young Middle Eastern nomad who has been sent away from the desert—and from his betrothed, Halima—against his will. While Atiyah studies the Koran, Halima is captured by another tribe of desert nomads. It falls to Atiyah and Etienne to rescue her.

425. Treece, Henry. *The Golden One*. Illus. William Stobbs. 1961. New York: Criterion, 1962. 191 pp. Junior.

Beginning in Byzantium in the year 1204, this story follows the children of a Viking who is a captain in the Varangian Guard. The children, Constantine and Theodora, must escape when the Franks attack; they end up with Genghis Khan.

426. Walsh, Jill Paton. *The Emperor's Winding Sheet*. New York: Farrar, Straus & Giroux, 1974. 274 pp. (0-374-32160-4 hc.) Junior.

Piers, a young man from Bristol, England, is captured by pirates and escapes to the Byzantine Empire. He ends up serving the emperor and is present when Constantinople falls to the Turks in 1453. Walsh deals convincingly with the linguistic difficulties Piers faces in a foreign land. Author's note.

CHAPTER TWELVE

Medieval Legends and Folklore

To cover all the books featuring medieval legend and folklore is far beyond the scope of this bibliography. Instead, this chapter reveals a few of the subjects that were popular in the Middle Ages, such as the French Reynard the Fox cycle, the German story of the Pied Piper of Hamelin, the Irish legends of Cuchulain, the Spanish stories about El Cid, the Norse tales of gods and goddesses, and the English romance heroes like King Horn. Unless they are part of anthologies, retellings of *Beowulf* and of Robin Hood are not mentioned here, since they have their own sections in chapters 5 and 7, respectively, and books about the legend of King Arthur and his knights can be found in chapter 13.

427. Anderson, Rachel. *Renard the Fox.* Illus. Bob Dewar. Oxford Myths and Legends. Oxford: Oxford University Press, 1986. 80 pp. (0-192-74129-2 hc.) Elementary.
A cycle of stories about the trickster Reynard the Fox circulated throughout Europe in the medieval period; they owe a great deal to Aesop's fables. The stories are best known in a French version; Marie de France, Geoffrey Chaucer, and other writers incorporated elements from the Reynard cycle into their own works. Anderson translates and adapts 12 stories from the French cycle.

428. Bartos-Höppner, Barbara. *The Pied Piper of Hamelin*. Illus. Annegert Fuchshuber. Trans. Anthea Bell. New York: Lippincott, 1985. 28 pp. (0-397-32240-2 lib. bdg.) Elementary.

A prose retelling of the 13th-century German legend, illustrated with bright paintings that do not mitigate the grimness of the tale. After many years, only two children return, one blind and one deaf, and neither can say what has happened to the other children.

429. Brown, Roy. *Reynard the Fox*. Illus. John Vernon Lord. Based on the version by Joseph Jacobs. New York: Abelard-Schuman, 1969. 96 pp. Elementary-Middle.

Brown retells 16 short animal stories from the Reynard cycle, many of them full of cruelty and violence, which Brown does not soften (he discusses this in his foreword). Appealing black and white woodcuts accompany the tales.

430. Buck, Alan. *The Hound of Culain*. Illus. Richard Bennett. New York: Lothrop, Lee & Shepard, 1938. 241 pp. Middle-Junior.

A retelling of the story of the Irish hero Cuchulain.

431. Burkert, Nancy Ekholm. *Valentine and Orson: Re-created as a Folk Play in Verse and Paintings*. New York: Farrar, Straus & Giroux, 1989. 48 pp. (0-374-38078-3 hc.) Elementary-Middle.

Taking the story of twin brothers raised separately (one by the king, one in the forest by a bear) from a medieval romance, Burkert retells it in confident iambic pentameter couplets. Her accompanying paintings (inspired by a design of Pieter Brueghel the Elder) tell a second story: the play of Valentine and Orson is performed by a troupe of 16th-century Flemish actors. Author's note.

432. Crossley-Holland, Kevin. *Havelok the Dane*. Illus. Brian Wildsmith. New York: Dutton, 1965. 178 pp. Middle-Junior.

Crossley-Holland turns the story of a king's son who is brought up by working people, but who wins his way back into the nobility again, into a novel. The original is a Middle English poetic romance.

433. ———. *King Horn: A Medieval Romance*. Illus. Charles Keeping. 1965. Ipswich, England: The Boydell Press, 1973. 215 pp. (0-85115-028-4 hc.) Junior-Senior.

This is a retelling of a 13th-century Middle English verse romance about an exiled prince, a love triangle, and battles against the Saracens. Crossley-Holland stays close to the original as he turns the poem into prose.

434. Czarnota, Lorna MacDonald. *Medieval Tales That Kids Can Read and Tell*. Little Rock: August House, 2000. 96 pp. (0-87483-589-5 hc.) Middle.

A storyteller presents 17 very short stories from medieval history and legend, along with tips for how to tell them. Episodes from the lives of Eleanor of Aquitaine and Joan of Arc, as well as excerpts from *Beowulf*, *The Song of Roland*, and tales from Switzerland, Poland, Greece, and Scotland, are included. The book ends with a chapter about storytelling and "How to be a Medieval Storyteller," including instructions for how to make a tunic. Bibliography, glossary.

435. D'Aulaire, Ingri, and Edgar Parin D'Aulaire. *D'Aulaires' Norse Gods and Giants*. New York: Doubleday, 1967. 163 pp. (0-385-23692-1 pb.) Elementary.

In this book, illustrated in bright colors with their characteristic technique of soft pencil drawings on stone, the D'Aulaires tell the stories of the creation and the end of the world, and much that happens in between amongst the gods and other creatures of Norse mythology. Introduction, glossary with pronunciation guide and literal meaning of words in Old Norse.

436. De Paola, Tomie, writer/illus. *Fin M'Coul: The Giant of Knockmany Hill*. New York: Holiday House, 1981. 32 pp. (0-8234-0384-X hc.) Elementary.

Using his characteristically warm palette and comical figures, de Paola retells an episode in the Cuchulain story in which Fin M'Coul's wife Oonagh saves the day. Patterns from Irish metalwork decorate the borders. Short author's note.

437. Ebbutt, M. I. *Hero-Myths and Legends of the British Race*. New York: Farrar and Rinehart, 1931. 374 pp. Middle.

Illustrated with 51 full-page illustrations by a variety of artists, this book retells the tales of several famous heroes including Beowulf, Havelok the Dane, Roland, Sir Gamelyn, King Horn, Robin Hood, Hereward the Wake, Cuchulain, and others less well-known. Glossary, index.

438. Frost, Abigail. *The Age of Chivalry (Myths and Legends)*. New York: Marshall Cavendish, 1990. 48 pp. (1-854-35235-0 lib. bdg.) Elementary-Middle.

Retellings of legends about Charlemagne and King Arthur.

439. Hastings, Selina. *Reynard the Fox*. Illus. Graham Percy. New York: Tambourine Books, 1990. 76 pp. (0-688-10156-9 lib. bdg.) Elementary.

Basing her retelling on William Caxton's 1481 printed version, Hastings combines several Reynard stories (see Anderson, above) into one continuous narrative for younger readers. Enchanting as they are, the sweet, soft colored-pencil illustrations, showing round-eyed animals in human clothing, sometimes belie the cruelty inherent in these stories.

440. Hodges, Margaret. *St. Jerome and the Lion*. Illus. Barry Moser. New York: Orchard Books, 1991. 32 pp. (0-531-08538-4 lib. bdg.) Elementary.

Jerome lived in the fourth and fifth centuries, so he is too early to be considered medieval. Yet he was so important for the medieval church that it seems right to include the legend of the saint, his dog, and his lion, particularly since it is so beautifully retold and illustrated here. Jerome lives in a monastery, laboring to translate the Bible into Latin, when a wounded lion appears. Everyone else runs in fear, but Jerome heals the lion, who becomes his companion—until the lion is accused of eating the monastery's donkey.

441. Holden, Robert. *The Pied Piper of Hamelin*. Illus. Drahos Zak. Boston: Houghton Mifflin, 1998. 32 pp. (0-395-89918-4 lib. bdg.) Elementary.

Zak's creepy, cartoon-like paintings are the raison d'être for this book; Holden's undistinguished text doesn't know whether it wants to be poetry or prose. There's no sugar-coated ending to the familiar story in Zak's illustrations—the last picture shows two crows in bare trees looking down on the town of Hamelin—but Holden leaves things more ambiguous, writing: "The children left singing for a future much brighter."

442. Jewett, Eleanore Myers. *Told on the King's Highway*. Illus. Marie A. Lawson. New York: Viking, 1943. 246 pp. Middle-Junior.

Jewett retells 16 medieval tales and adds a note about her sources.

443. Koenig, Alma Johanna. *Gudrun*. 1928. Trans. from German by
    Anthea Bell. New York: Lothrop, Lee & Shepard, 1979. 187 pp.
    (0-688-51899-0 lib. bdg.) Junior-Senior.
This prose retelling of a 13th-century Middle High German heroic
poem was written by a woman who died in a Nazi concentration camp.
A minstrel prophesies that Gudrun, the daughter of a king, will have
beauty, constancy, and grief, all of which come true. After she is betrothed to Herwig, Gudrun is kidnapped by a rejected suitor and held
captive. The tale has strong female characters, along with fairy-tale elements like a speaking swan. Translator's note.

444. Lewis, Naomi. *Proud Knight, Fair Lady: The 12 Lais of Marie de
    France*. Illus. Angela Barrett. New York: Viking Kestrel, 1989. 100
    pp. (0-670-82656-1 hc.) Middle.
The 12th-century writer Marie de France lived in Norman England and
wrote these *lais* in French poetry. Most of them are about love, and elements of the supernatural appear, such as a noble werewolf, a knight
who transforms into a bird, and a fairy queen who takes one of King
Arthur's knights as her lover. Lewis retells the *lais* in prose, illustrated
by Barrett's full-color paintings and decorations. A substantial introduction is included.

445. McCaughrean, Geraldine. *El Cid*. Illus. Victor Ambrus. Oxford:
    Oxford University Press, 1988. 128 pp. (0-19-276007-7 hc.) Middle.
A retelling of the 12th-century poem celebrating an 11th-century
Spanish hero who was first banished by the king, and then won Valen-
cia back from Moorish occupation. Stirring full-page illustrations with
plenty of yellows and reds evoke medieval Spain and complement the
short prose chapters.

446. Middleton, Hadyn. *Island of the Mighty: Stories of Old Britain*. Illus.
    Anthea Toorchen. Oxford Myths and Legends. Oxford: Oxford Uni-
    versity Press, 1987. 80 pp. (0-19-274133-0 hc.) Elementary.
Most of the five stories of Celtic kings, giants, dragons, and magic in
this collection are taken from "The Mabinogion," a collection of Welsh
stories about gods, goddesses, heroes, and magic which were passed
down orally for countless generations before they were written down in
the 13th century. However, Middleton does not reveal his sources in
this book. Full-color watercolors accompany the text.

447. Nye, Robert. *Taliesin*. Illus. Dorothy Mass. New York: Hill and
     Wang, 1966. 126 pp. Middle-Junior.
Nye retells the story from "The Mabinogion" of the peasant boy Gwion
who tasted the witch's brew and became the great poet Taliesin. Although he had to be reborn and live through childhood all over again,
this time he came into the world speaking poetry. Simple pen and ink
illustrations accompany the text.

448. Osborne, Mary Pope. *Favorite Medieval Tales*. Illus. Troy Howell.
     New York: Scholastic, 1998. 86 pp. (0-590-60042-7 hc.) Elemen-
     tary-Middle.
The introduction tells how language has changed in England, and
each tale begins with a quotation from the original language. The
nine tales, "Finn Maccoul," "Beowulf," "The Sword in the Stone,"
"Island of the Lost Children" (from the Middle High German *Gudrun*), "The Song of Roland," "The Werewolf" (by Marie de France),
"Sir Gawain and the Green Knight," "Robin Hood and His Merry
Men," and "Chanticleer and the Fox," are each illustrated with an illuminated title page and a full-page painting. Notes, chronology,
bibliography, index.

449. ———. *Favorite Norse Myths*. Illus. Troy Howell. New York:
     Scholastic, 1996. 88 pp. (0-590-48046-4 hc.) Elementary-Middle.
Osborne retells stories from the Elder and Younger Eddas in clear, el-
egant prose, and enticing quotations from the Poetic Edda begin several chapters. Howell's gorgeous acrylic and oil paintings have designs from early Norse art scratched into them; you can find the same
design at the beginning of the chapter the painting illustrates. An
introduction and author's note help to set the stories within their
historical and literary context. Glossary, bibliography, artist's note,
index.

450. Pilkington, F. M. *The Three Sorrowful Tales of Erin*. Illus. Victor
     Ambrus. New York: Henry Z. Walck, 1966. 232 pp. Middle-Junior.
These Irish poems, passed down orally for centuries, were probably
written down in the ninth century; here Pilkington uses prose to retell
"The Fate of the Children of Tuireann," "The Fate of the Children of
Lir," and "Deirdre and the Sons of Uisne." Ambrus's black and white
drawings appear every few pages. Author's note.

451. Serraillier, Ian. *Havelok the Dane*. Illus. Elaine Raphael. New York: Henry Z. Walck, 1967. 67 pp. Middle-Junior.
Serraillier retells the early Middle English metrical romance about a dispossessed prince, brought up by fishermen, who wins the hand of the princess.

452. Sutcliff, Rosemary. *The Hound of Ulster*. Illus. Victor Ambrus. New York: Dutton, 1963. 192 pp. Middle-Junior.
Sutcliff retells the story of the Irish hero Cuchulain in the form of a novel, although her prose remains stately, as befits the epic tale. Ambrus's black and white drawings are mainly used at the beginnings of new chapters. Author's note.

453. Thomas, Gwyn, and Kevin Crossley-Holland. *Tales from the Mabinogion*. Illus. Margaret Jones. Woodstock, NY: Overlook Press, 1985. 87 pp. (0-87951-978-8 hc.) Elementary.
Thomas, a renowned scholar of Welsh, works with Crossley-Holland to retell four branches of "The Mabinogion" (Pwyll, Branwen, Manawydan, and Math) for young readers. The artist incorporates Celtic patterns into her attractive paintings and drawings. Glossary and pronunciation guide of Welsh names.

454. Westwood, Jennifer. *Medieval Tales*. Illus. Pauline Baynes. New York: Coward-McCann, 1967. 148 pp. Middle-Junior.
Here be dragons—as well as Chaucer's Chanticleer, and Ysengrin the Wolf, Aucassin and Nicolette, Sir Orfeo, Sir Gawain and the Green Knight, and other medieval tales, 16 in all. Five *Canterbury Tales* are retold: the Nun's Priest's, the Wife of Bath's, the Pardoner's, the Friar's, and the Canon's Yeoman's, although they aren't identified as such within the text. Instead, Westwood calls them "The Loathly Lady," "The Devil and the Summoner," etc. Then, in her long author's note, she explains the genre and author—if one is known—of each of her stories.

455. Williams, Jay. *The Horn of Roland*. Illus. Sean Morrison. New York: Thomas Crowell, 1968. 157 pp. Middle-Junior.
Williams turns the 11th-century *Song of Roland*, which celebrates events from Charlemagne's reign, two centuries before, into a novel. His author's note explains the variety of French chansons de geste and

English romances he relied on as sources. Morrison's precise pencil drawings complement the tale.

456. ———. *The Tournament of the Lions.* Illus. Ezra Jack Keats. New York: Henry Z. Walck, 1960. 120 pp. Middle.

Williams sets this prose retelling of *The Song of Roland* at a 15th-century tournament held by the historical figure Rene of Anjou. Two squires attending the tournament do not know the story, and an old knight tells it to them. As readers encounter the story, they also learn about 15th-century knights, castle life, and tournaments. A stylized black and white illustration accompanies each chapter. Glossary, author's note.

CHAPTER THIRTEEN

Arthurian Legend

Many people think of Arthur as an English king, but Arthurian literature is international in scope. France and Germany, in particular, have strong traditions of Arthurian literature, as some of the entries below indicate; the *Parzival* that Katherine Paterson retells is a Middle High German poem, for example. Meanwhile, Kevin Crossley-Holland turns to Sir Thomas Malory's English *Morte Darthur*, but Malory used both French and English sources as he wrote his great work.

Did King Arthur really exist? Certainly not as we imagine him, as a king in a chivalric setting surrounded by knights wearing 14th-century armor. If he lived at all, he would have been either Roman or British, not English. In fact, as a survivor of the Romano-British people who defended the land against the invading Anglo-Saxons in the fifth century, he would have been the enemy of the English. He could have been a Roman military leader. More likely, he was probably a hero of legend, the kind of hero we would *like* to have existed.

Because Cindy Mediavilla's *Arthurian Fiction: An Annotated Bibliography* covers books for middle school through adult readers, I do not duplicate her work. Instead in this section I mention some Arthurian titles that either did not belong in her book or that were published too recently to be included in it. Except for Crossley-Holland's trilogy, none of the books listed below could be considered historical fiction; instead, they incorporate tales of magic and the supernatural, as did medieval Arthurian legends. They tell us about the kinds of entertainments medieval audiences enjoyed, but they shouldn't be taken as reflections of how people lived in the Middle Ages any more than readers 500 years from now should try to chart our daily lives from a reading of Lois Lowry's *The Giver*.

457. Crossley-Holland, Kevin. Arthur Trilogy: Book 1. *The Seeing Stone*. New York: Arthur A. Levine / Scholastic, 2001. 342 pp. (0-439-26326-3 hc.) Middle-Junior.

A splendid evocation of life on a 12th-century English manor, told through the eyes of a 13-year-old boy named Arthur. Although his visions of King Arthur (all taken from medieval sources) add a fantasy element to the novel, the setting of the main story is historical, not fantastic. In the 100 short chapters, readers learn the legend of the king through the protagonist's visions. Glossary. Smarties Bronze Medal, Shortlisted for Whitbread Award.

458. ———. Arthur Trilogy: Book 2. *At the Crossing Places*. New York: Arthur A. Levine / Scholastic, 2002. 394 pp. (0-439-26598-3 hc.) Middle-Junior.

Picking up where the first book ended, Arthur continues his visions of the legendary king while he becomes a squire to Lord Stephen, a Crusader knight, and struggles with the question of his true parentage. Glossary.

459. ———. Arthur Trilogy: Book 3. *King of the Middle March*. London: Orion Children's Books, 2003. 432 pp. (1-842-55060-8 hc.) New York: Arthur A. Levine / Scholastic, 2004. Middle-Junior.

In 1201, Arthur the squire accompanies Lord Stephen to Venice to prepare for the Fourth Crusade, and then on to the Holy Land. Two years later he returns home with mixed feelings about war—both the Crusaders' wars and those of King Arthur, whose story the seeing stone shows him. Meanwhile, his difficult family relationships continue and his betrothal looms.

460. ———. *The World of King Arthur and His Court: People, Places, Legend, and Lore*. Illus. Peter Malone. New York: Dutton, 1999. 125 pp. (0-525-46167-1 hc.) Elementary-Middle.

An anthology of short (one to three page) passages about knighthood, medieval life, King Arthur, and the people and stories associated with him. Some passages are quotations from medieval texts; in others, Crossley-Holland briefly tells readers about a topic like the Crusades or tournaments or Merlin.

461. Hastings, Selina. *Sir Gawain and the Green Knight.* Illus. Juan Wijngaard. New York: Lothrop, Lee & Shepard, 1981. 28 pp. (0-688-00592-6 hc.) Elementary.

Hastings retells the 14th-century Middle English poem in prose, sticking closely to its plot—Sir Gawain accepts the unearthly Green Knight's challenge, an exchange of blows. Sir Gawain cuts off the Green Knight's head, but in a year he must offer the Green Knight his own head. Wijngaard's illustrations and decorations add other details from the poem that don't appear in the text.

462. ———. *Sir Gawain and the Loathly Lady.* Illus. Juan Wijngaard. New York: Lothrop, Lee & Shepard, 1985. 32 pp. (0-688-05823-X hc.) Elementary.

Sumptuous illustrations and illuminated borders inspired by medieval manuscripts enhance this retelling of a tale similar to *The Wife of Bath's Tale.* The story revolves around the question of what women want most. To save King Arthur's honor, Sir Gawain must marry a monstrously ugly woman—who ends up being a beautiful woman under a spell.

463. Morris, Gerald *Parsifal's Page.* Boston: Houghton Mifflin, 2001. 232 pp. (0-618-05509-6 hc.) Junior.

The fourth book in Morris's series, (which begins with *The Squire's Tale*) based on Wolfram von Eschenbach's *Parzival*, tells the story of an 11-year-old boy, Piers, who becomes Parsifal's page. Terence and Gawain again play a role.

464. ———. *The Savage Damsel and the Dwarf.* Boston: Houghton Mifflin, 2000. 213 pp. (0-395-97126-8 hc.) Junior.

Terence and Sir Gawain return in the third volume. However, this story really belongs to a young woman, Lynet, and is based on Malory's "Tale of Sir Gareth of Orkney that was called Beaumains."

465. ———. *The Squire, His Knight, and His Lady.* Boston: Houghton Mifflin, 1999. 232 pp. (0-395-91211-3 hc.) Junior.

The adventures of Terence and Sir Gawain continue in this book, which is inspired by the 14th-century poem *Sir Gawain and the Green Knight*.

466. ———. *The Squire's Tale*. Boston: Houghton Mifflin, 1998. 212 pp. (0-395-86959-9 hc.) Junior.

Morris draws on Malory's *Morte Darthur* in this delightful tale of Sir Gawain and his squire, Terence (Morris's invention), a 14-year-old boy with magical powers. Sir Gawain is heroic in this telling. The setting for all of Morris's Arthurian books is not medieval; rather, it's the same kind of setting you find in medieval romances, where a hermit can remember the future but not the past (in an unacknowledged borrowing from T. H. White's *The Once and Future King*), and where Terence can see fairies.

467. O'Neal, Michael. *King Arthur: Opposing Viewpoints*. San Diego: Greenhaven Press, 1992. 112 pp. (0-89908-095-2 hc.) Junior-Senior.

Tracing the medieval origins of the Arthurian legend through its various sources and summarizing Malory's version of the tale, O'Neal provides readers with enough information to help them understand that some parts of the Arthurian story may be based in reality while other parts are clearly the stuff of legend. Black and white illustrations, many of them 19th-century renderings, are included. Glossary, bibliography, index.

468. Paterson, Katherine. *Parzival: The Quest of the Grail Knight*. New York: Dutton, 1998. 129 pp. (0-525-67579-5 hc.) Middle-Junior.

A retelling of Wolfram von Eschenbach's 13th-century German story of the Grail knight, in the form of a novel. Parzival knows nothing of his heritage, but as a boy he is enchanted by King Arthur's knights. Moving from ignorance to wisdom, he becomes the best of Arthur's knights. Author's note.

469. Serraillier, Ian. *The Challenge of the Green Knight*. Illus. Victor Ambrus. New York: Henry Z. Walck, 1967. 56 pp. Middle-Junior.

A retelling of the Middle English poem *Sir Gawain and the Green Knight*, illustrated in black and white.

470. Sutcliff, Rosemary. *Tristan and Iseult*. New York: Dutton, 1971. 150 pp. (0-525-41565-3 hc.) Junior-Senior.

The doomed love affair of Tristan, one of King Arthur's knights, and Iseult, who was married to King Marc of Cornwall, is retold in prose, but Sutcliff leaves many elements as unexplained as they are in the 12th-century German poem, keeping the work's folkloric quality. The major change she has made, which she explains in her foreword, is eliminating the potion that makes Tristan and Iseult fall in love with each other; Sutcliff makes her lovers more culpable.

CHAPTER FOURTEEN

Professional Resources for Educators

Books, Periodicals, Articles, and ERIC Documents

The variety of resources available for educators indicates the interdisciplinary nature of studying the Middle Ages. Many of the articles and books mentioned in this section describe classroom activities that encompass many disciplines, including literature, writing, visual arts, history and social studies, math, science, foreign languages, and music. ERIC Documents are indicated by "ED" followed by a number.

471. Adamson, Lynda G. *Recreating the Past: A Guide to American and World Historical Fiction for Children and Young Adults*. Westport, CT: Greenwood, 1994.

This useful annotated bibliography has a very broad scope, but it helpfully classifies works by time period and geographical location. Some of the works included under the medieval period are fantasy, not historical fiction. Oddly, each entry ends with a suggested moral for the work.

472. Adkins, Chandra Lynn Power. *Presentism or Plausible Past? The Selective Tradition in Historical Fiction Written for Young People*. PhD dissertation. University of Georgia, 1998. UMI 9836933.

In this unpublished dissertation, available online from Dissertation Abstracts International or in print from University Microfilms International,

Adkins looks at the ways both writers and readers impose modern values onto past eras when they read or write about them. Adkins includes analyses of Cushman's *Catherine, Called Birdy*, Temple's *The Ramsay Scallop*, Tomlinson's *The Forestwife*, Garden's *Dove and Sword: A Novel of Joan of Arc*, and Bradford's *There Will Be Wolves*.

473. Aiken, Joan. "Interpreting the Past." *Children's Literature in Education* 16 (Summer 1985): 67–83.

Although this article isn't specifically about historical fiction of the Middle Ages, Aiken explores the different ways adults and children respond to history and historical fiction. Her thoughtful discussion gives suggestions about ways writers can present the past to young readers.

474. Atterton, Julian. "Plain Tales from the North." *Children's Literature in Education* 18.2 (Summer 1987): 113–121.

A writer of historical novels for adolescents discusses why he chose to write about the Middle Ages and the kinds of problems and decisions he faces as a writer of historical fiction.

475. Barnhouse, Rebecca. "Books and Reading in Adolescent Literature Set in the Middle Ages." *The Lion and the Unicorn* 22 (1998): 364–375.

This article focuses on Bradford's *There Will Be Wolves*, Garden's *Dove and Sword: A Novel of Joan of Arc*, and Cushman's *Catherine, Called Birdy* and *The Midwife's Apprentice* to show the ways historical novelists represent—or misrepresent—medieval literacy, often allowing modern attitudes about the importance of books and reading to creep into their fiction.

476. ———. "Leeches and Leprosy: Medieval Medicine in Modern Novels for Young Readers." *Literature and Medicine* 21.1 (Spring 2002): 26–44.

This article uses six novels to show the ways medieval medicine has been portrayed by modern writers, particularly focusing on the close connection between Christianity, illness, and healing in the Middle Ages. Older novels—de Angeli's *The Door in the Wall*, Sutcliff's *The Witch's Brat*, Trease's *The Red Towers of Granada*—are compared with more recent fiction: Bradford's *There Will Be Wolves*, Garden's *Dove and Sword: A Novel of Joan of Arc*, and Cushman's *Matilda Bone*.

477. ———. "The Pleasure of Discovery: Medieval Literature in Adolescent Novels Set in the Middle Ages." *ALAN Review* 26.2 (Winter 1999): 53–57.

Many authors include medieval literature within their novels, and this article examines a variety of ways well-known works such as *Beowulf*, *The Canterbury Tales*, and *The Song of Roland* and lesser-known works such as *The Anglo-Saxon Chronicle* have been incorporated into fiction. Temple's *The Ramsay Scallop*, Alder's *The King's Shadow*, Stolz's *Pangur Ban*, Cadnum's *In a Dark Wood*, and Paterson's *Parzival: The Quest of a Grail Knight* are discussed, and the article ends with suggestions for classroom activities.

478. ———. *Recasting the Past: The Middle Ages in Young Adult Literature.* Portsmouth, NH: Heinemann / Boynton Cook, 2000.

Written mainly for middle school and junior and senior high school teachers, this book focuses on 19 novels, evaluating them for historical accuracy and setting the works within their historical context. It also briefly teaches readers about various aspects of the medieval period. Suggestions for classroom use are offered.

479. ———. "Robin Hood Comes of Age." *ALAN Review* 30.2 (Winter 2003): 25–29.

A history of the legend in both English literature and children's literature is followed by a look at recent Robin Hood novels. Some, like Michael Cadnum's works, are historical fiction; others, like Nancy Springer's *Rowan Hood: Outlaw Girl of Sherwood Forest*, are fantasy; and still others, like Tomlinson's *The Forestwife*, exist somewhere between fantasy and historical fiction.

480. Beidler, Peter G. "Low-Tech Chaucer: An Experimental Iambic Pentameter Creative Project." *Exercise Exchange* 46.1 (Fall 2000): 16–20.

High school students learn about Chaucer's iambic pentameter by writing their own rhyming couplets in Modern English. Three projects of increasing length are described here.

481. Blishen, Edward, ed. *The Thorny Paradise: Writers on Writing for Children.* Harmondsworth: Penguin Books, 1975.

Although none of them specifically discuss novels set in the Middle Ages, 6 of the 22 authors whose short essays about their influences, the writing process, or children's literature are included here write historical fiction about the medieval period: Geoffrey Trease, C. Walter Hodges, Jill Paton Walsh, Rosemary Sutcliff, Ian Serraillier, and Barbara Willard.

482. Bourgeault, Cynthia. "Medieval Religious Drama: Riches for Reclamation." *Momentum* 9.3 (Oct 1978): 17–22.

Looking at both the history and the availability of material for medieval drama, Bourgeault makes a case for its production at the high school level.

483. Brockman, Bennett. "Robin Hood and the Invention of Children's Literature." *Children's Literature* 10 (1982): 1–17.

Beginning with an overview about the way the Robin Hood legend has been presented over the centuries, Brockman argues that by the Renaissance, the medieval romance had become devalued, and the audience for it had changed from adults to children and the lower classes. Because the Robin Hood stories were part of the romance tradition, they became associated with children's literature.

484. Brown, J. "Into the Minds of Babes: Children's Books and the Past." In *Presenting the Past: Essays on History and the Public*, ed. S. P. Benson, et al. Philadelphia: Temple University Press, 1986: 67–84.

An academic historian explores the issues of presenting history to children through literature. He praises Macaulay's *Cathedral*, *Castle*, and other titles for showing how the construction of these buildings is tied in with the "social relations" of the town, making them books full of complex ideas. The article does not focus on the Middle Ages but concerns itself with a wide variety of literature about history.

485. Budd, Kelly, and Jayne Alexander. "Arthurian Legends and the Medieval Period for Grade 9 Study." ED 413599. 1997.

In this unit, students compare various versions of the Arthurian legends, work in small groups on writing and art projects, and watch the film *Ladyhawke*. Some material from unidentified sources is reproduced in this unit.

486. *Calliope: The World History Magazine*, for grades four and above (ages 9–14), has several issues on medieval topics.

Each issue has 52 pages and includes articles, maps, time lines, and art-work. An e-mail address invites students to ask questions about world history. The website gives tips for incorporating the magazine into lesson plans. Back issues are available from Cobblestone Publishing ($4.95 each) at www.cobblestonepub.com. The text of this journal is also available electronically through subscribing libraries. Back issues about the Middle Ages include: The Black Death; Byzantium, Constantinople, Istanbul; Charlemagne; Children of the Middle Ages; The First Crusade; Defenders of France; Gutenberg and Printing; Ibn Battuta: Moslem Traveler; Islamic Spain; Magna Carta; Monasteries in Medieval Europe; Norman Conquest; Norse Gods; and Vikings.

487. Carter, John Marshall. "Classroom Ideas: The Bayeux Tapestry in the Social Studies Class." *Social Education* 50.4 (Apr–May 1986): 314–316.
Carter offers ideas for integrating writing and other activities about the 11th century into middle and senior high school classrooms.

488. *Children's Literature Association Quarterly* 8.2 (Summer 1983).
This issue is devoted to historical fiction for children and includes John Cech's "Pyle's Robin Hood: Still Merry after All These Years" (11–14).

489. Christensen, Lois M. "Symbols and Scrolls: Teaching Elementary Students about Historic Writing." *Social Studies and the Young Learner* 12.1 (Sept–Oct 1999): 5–8.
Christensen describes a hands-on unit about the history of writing from the ancient period to the Middle Ages. Students conduct research and practice writing styles.

490. Crew, Adolph B. "Life in a Monastery: A Unit in Group Creativity." *Social Studies* 75.6 (Nov–Dec 1984): 273–275.
Crew describes how seventh-grade students turned their classroom into a monastery as they studied medieval religion.

491. Downs, Anita. "Breathing Life in the Past: The Creation of History Units Using Trade Books." In *The Story of Ourselves: Teaching History through Children's Literature*, ed. Michael O. Tunnell and Richard Ammon. Portsmouth, NH: Heinemann, 1993: 137–145.
Downs describes activities she uses with fourth graders to make history more interesting. Her interdisciplinary unit on "Castles and Castle

Times" incorporates trade books, small-group research projects, and group presentations.

492. Drake, Susan M. "Castles, Kings . . . and Standards." *Educational Leadership* 59.1 (Sept 2001): 38–42.
A fourth-grade teacher describes a multidisciplinary unit based around a medieval fair and involving history, science, language arts, and fine arts.

493. Fisher, Janet. *An Index to Historical Fiction for Children and Young People*. Aldershot, England: Scolar Press and Brookfield, VT: Ashgate, 1994.
In this useful annotated bibliography, the focus is on British works. Fisher naturally expects her audience to be familiar with British history, so American readers might have to look up some of the dates or events she refers to.

494. Fitzhugh, Mike. "Medieval Theatre: It's More Fun Than It Looks." *Teaching Theatre* 7.4 (Summer 1996): 13–16.
Fitzhugh discusses the production of plays like the "Wakefield Noah" and lists some of the concerns that need to be addressed before undertaking medieval drama.

495. Ford, Miriam R. "Banners and Hangings." *School Arts* 72.8 (Apr 1973): 46–47.
Sixth-grade social studies students create banners as part of their study of the Middle Ages.

496. Goodwin, Meredyth L. "*Beowulf* and the Warriors." *English Journal* 72 (1983): 36–37.
Goodwin writes about helping Native American students learn to appreciate the poem, and at the same time, helping a colleague overcome his prejudices towards his Native American students.

497. Hardwick, Paul. "'Not in the Middle Ages?' Alan Garner's *The Owl Service* and the Literature of Adolescence." *Children's Literature in Education* 31.1 (Mar 2000): 23–30.
Hardwick discusses 19th-century and more recent constructs of the Middle Ages. He compares a "safe medievalism" found in Roger Lancelyn Green's use of the Legend of the Sleepers with Alan Garner's use of the same legend to create tension.

498. Harty, Kevin. *The Reel Middle Ages: Films about Medieval Europe.* Jefferson, NC: McFarland, 1999.
This filmography gives a synopsis, a cast list, and references for reviews of films made in North America, Europe, and Asia.

499. Hicks, Alun, and Dave Martin. *Teaching English and History: Reading and Writing Historical Fiction.* Dorset Education Professional Development Services, 1994. ISBN: 0-85216-698-2.
Obtainable from Dorset Education, Professional Development Services, County Hall, Dorchester, Dorset, England DT1 1XJ. A longer study of the project described in the following entry.

500. ———. "Teaching English and History through Historical Fiction." *Children's Literature in Education* 28 (1997): 49–59.
Two British teachers ask readers to consider exactly what defines historical novels. Then they look at the ways the historical novel can fit into a school curriculum, focusing on a unit on medieval England. Using McCaughrean's *A Little Lower Than the Angels* as their text, and comparing it to novels by Geoffrey Trease and Rosemary Sutcliff, their students write their own historical fiction, and Hicks and Martin give useful suggestions for classroom activities.

501. Himmell, Rhoda. "The Role of Women in Medieval Europe: A Unit of Study for Grades 10–12." ED 377118. 1992.
This 70-page document describes a unit prepared at the National Center for History in the Schools, sponsored by the National Endowment for the Humanities. Students focus on women's roles in several areas: the early Germanic tribes during the time that the Roman Empire was breaking apart; the feudal era; the cultural and intellectual milieu of the high Middle Ages; and occupational roles in the late Middle Ages. Activities include role-playing.

502. Hinelin, Catherine Almy. "*Beowulf* as History, as Saga, as Monster." *Independent School* 38 (1978): 25–28.
Fourth- and fifth-grade students read *Beowulf* and participate in activities based on it during a unit on Anglo-Saxon England.

503. Honan, Linda. *Picture the Middle Ages.* Illus. Ellen Kosmer. Amawalk, NY: Golden Owl, 1994. Reprint 1996. (1-56696-025-8 spiral bound.)

A resource book with reproducible material including drawings, a time line, word games, and music. Although the book is intended for a five-to-eight-week "unit on the Middle Ages" for upper elementary and middle schools, it's a valuable supplement for anyone teaching medieval history, music, clothing and armor, or art, and it includes ideas for putting on medieval festivals, feasts, or fairs. The book is available from Jackdaw Publications, www.jackdaw.com.

504. *Jackdaws*. Amawalk, NY: Jackdaw Publications.
These historical-document portfolios for grades 7–12 include a variety of reproductions of primary sources and documents for use on a particular theme, as well as a study guide, lesson plans, and reproducible material. For example, the Alfred the Great portfolio includes "broadsheets" with information about King Alfred's life and reign, and about the complexity of source material from ninth-century England. Also included are a map of Anglo-Saxon England, manuscript pages, translations of key texts like Alfred's introduction to the *Pastoral Care*, *The Anglo-Saxon Chronicle*, and the treaty between Alfred and the Danes, as well as pictures of art, architecture, jewelry, coins, and ships from Alfred's time. Other medieval subjects covered by *Jackdaws* include: 1066; The Black Death; The Byzantine Empire: A Cultural Legacy; Joan of Arc; Magna Carta; The Peasants' Revolt; The Spanish Inquisition; and The Vikings. Two *Jackdaws* cover the history of writing: "The Development of Writing" is for grades 7–12, while a simpler version, "Cave Paintings to Printing Presses" is geared at grades 5–8. Each portfolio costs $42. For ordering information, as well as specifics about what each portfolio contains, see www.jackdaw.com.

505. Keenan, Celia. "Reflecting a New Confidence: Irish Historical Fiction for Children." *The Lion and the Unicorn* 21 (1997): 369–378.
Discussing historical fiction in general and Irish history specifically, Keenan alerts readers to some of the problems and possibilities writers encounter when they choose historical fiction to tell their stories. Books with medieval settings that Keenan includes in her discussion are Michael Mullen's *Sea Wolves from the North*, Morgan Llywelyn's *Strongbow*, and Maeve Friel's historical fantasy *Distant Voices*.

506. MacLeod, Anne Scott. "Howard Pyle's Robin Hood: The Middle Ages for Americans." *Children's Literature Association Quarterly* 25.1 (Spring 2000): 44–48.

MacLeod explores the cultural milieu in which Pyle's *Robin Hood* was published (in 1883) and the ways that fin de siècle culture embraced a view of the Middle Ages as passionate, wholesome, and heroic, qualities many felt their own time sorely lacked. MacLeod suggests that this cultural "disquiet" may explain the popularity of Pyle's stories of a romanticized past.

507. ———. "Writing Backwards: Modern Models in Historical Fiction." *Horn Book* 74 (Jan–Feb 1998): 26–33.
MacLeod argues that many recent historical novels, including Cushman's *Catherine, Called Birdy*, portray heroines as having modern values and choices, not those that would have been available during the actual time period in which the books are set.

508. Margolis, S. "Breathing Life into the Middle Ages for Young Adults." *School Library Journal* 42 (1996): 36–37.
Margolis gives paragraph-long summaries of 13 novels set in the English Middle Ages, including Sutcliff's *The Witch's Brat*, Cushman's *The Midwife's Apprentice*, Konigsburg's *A Proud Taste for Scarlet and Miniver*, Gray's *Adam of the Road*, Garden's *Dove and Sword*, McKinley's *Outlaws of Sherwood*, and Tomlinson's *The Forestwife*.

509. May, Jill. "The Hero's Woods: Pyle's *Robin Hood* and the Female Reader." *Children's Literature Association Quarterly* 11.4 (Winter 1986–1987): 197–200.
Recalling her childhood ability to play-act Robin Hood stories—despite their lack of active female characters—because of their sense of adventure and their romantic setting, a forest "where nature is gentle and supportive" (200), May argues that Pyle's *Robin Hood* appeals to both sexes.

510. McNulty, Mary H. "The Girls' Story: Adolescent Novels Set in the Middle Ages." *ALAN Review* 28.2 (Winter 2001): 20–23.
Noting that until the 1980s novels set in the Middle Ages tended to feature boys, McNulty discusses problems with authenticity when girls are the main characters. She focuses on seven novels: Cushman's *Catherine, Called Birdy*, *The Midwife's Apprentice*, and *Matilda Bone*; McGraw's *The Striped Ships*; McKinley's *Outlaws of Sherwood*; and Tomlinson's *The Forestwife* and *Child of the May*.

511. Mediavilla, Cindy. *Arthurian Fiction: An Annotated Bibliography*. Lanham, MD: Scarecrow, 1999.

Mediavilla provides in-depth summaries—along with evaluations of quality—of over 200 novels appropriate for middle-grade, young adult, and adult readers, organized around themes such as "Arthur, the Roman Leader" and "The Women of Camelot." The book begins with a very brief but helpful history of the Arthurian legend.

512. Meek, Margaret. *Rosemary Sutcliff*. New York: Walck, 1962.

In her short (72-page) literary biography, Meek discusses the historical fiction Sutcliff had written by 1960, including *Knight's Fee* and *The Shield Ring*, comparing Sutcliff's methods with those of other novelists. Meek wrote a similar volume about Geoffrey Trease (Walck, 1964).

513. Miller, Miriam Y. "Illustrations of *The Canterbury Tales* for Children: A Mirror of Chaucer's World." *Chaucer Review* 27.3 (1993): 293–304.

In this scholarly article, in which she explores the history of picture-book illustration, Miller, a medievalist, examines 19th- and 20th-century illustrations of Chaucer and their sources, looking to see which are inspired by medieval art. She finds that most illustrators prefer contemporary artistic conventions to medieval ones.

514. ———. "'The Rhythm of a Tongue': Literary Dialect in Rosemary Sutcliff's Novels of the Middle Ages for Children." *Children's Literature Association Quarterly* 19 (1994): 25–31.

Miller expertly explores the ways writers use language, and particularly dialogue, to make their books seem authentic, focusing on Sutcliff's *The Shield Ring*, *Knight's Fee*, and *The Witch's Brat*.

515. ———. "'Thy Speech Is Strange and Uncouth': Language in the Children's Historical Novel of the Middle Ages." *Children's Literature* 23 (1995): 71–90.

In this fascinating and highly informative discussion of the ways writers deal with the differences between medieval and modern languages, as well as with linguistic variety during the Middle Ages, Miller describes archaisms and "pseudo-archaisms," historical accuracy, and the ways writers appeal to children through dialogue. She focuses specifically on Trease's *Bows against the Barons*, de Angeli's *The Door in the Wall*, Gray's

Adam of the Road, Clements's *Prison Window, Jerusalem Blue*, Walsh's *The Emperor's Winding Sheet*, and the novels of Cynthia Harnett.

516. Mills, Alice. "Two Versions of Beowulf." *Children's Literature in Education* 17 (1986): 75–87.

Looking at Rosemary Sutcliff's *Dragonslayer* and Kevin Crossley-Holland's *Beowulf*, both illustrated by Charles Keeping, Mills compares the changes each author makes in the text and looks at Keeping's development as an artist from 1961 to 1982. Mills argues that Sutcliff weakens the poem by diminishing the monsters and the folkloric aspects in order to make it more realistic. She prefers Crossley-Holland's version, which cleaves more closely to the original poem.

517. Milosh, Joseph. "A Supplement for Teaching *Beowulf*." *English Journal* 59 (1970): 646–654.

Milosh describes activities for high school students who have already read the poem. They learn about Old English language and poetic techniques by translating and analyzing lines from the poem and imitating elements of Anglo-Saxon poetry in Modern English.

518. Modern Language Association (MLA) *Approaches to Teaching* . This series, while designed for college teachers, provides useful information that can be adapted to junior and senior high school classrooms.

In short articles, scholars discuss texts, teaching aids, and classroom approaches. Medieval subjects include the Arthurian tradition; *Beowulf*; Chaucer's *Canterbury Tales*; Dante's *Divine Comedy*; medieval English drama; and *Sir Gawain and the Green Knight*.

519. Olton, Bert. *Arthurian Legends on Film and Television*. Jefferson, NC: McFarland, 2000.

Olton's filmography contains synopses, as well as cast lists and credits.

520. Patrick, Mary. "Research without Revolt: Organizing a Banquet to Study the Medieval Period." *Gifted Child Today Magazine* 17.6 (Nov–Dec 1994): 34–35, 38.

Instead of writing research papers, high school seniors researched and planned a banquet.

521. Petry, Karla L. "*La Chanson de Roland* in the Elementary School Classroom: A Case for Medieval Literature and Young Language

Students." *Modern Language Journal* 65.2 (Summer 1981): 137–140.
Elementary school students in the Cincinnati public schools who were studying French got a combined lesson in literature, social studies, history, and language as they studied the Old French poem.

522. Raggio, Susan, and Dorothy Zjawin. "Knights in White Sneakers." *Instructor* 92.4 (Nov–Dec 1982): 34–37.
The authors describe a unit about medieval daily life, including social structure, agriculture, and feudalism. They give instructions for building a replica of a medieval village.

523. Rahn, Suzanne. "An Evolving Past: The Story of Historical Fiction and Nonfiction for Children." *The Lion and the Unicorn* 15 (1991): 1–26.
Rahn defines and surveys historical fiction in the 19th and 20th centuries, showing its connections with other genres—adventure stories, romances, detective stories, and fantasies—and its shift in audience and protagonists from just boys to girls, as well. Among the writers discussed are Elizabeth Janet Gray and Geoffrey Trease.

524. ———. "'It Would Be Awful Not to Know Greek': Rediscovering Geoffrey Trease." *The Lion and the Unicorn* 14 (1990): 23–52.
In her biographical overview of Trease and his works, Rahn discusses how he came to write his Robin Hood novel, *Bows against the Barons*.

525. Ranta, Taimi. "Howard Pyle's *The Merry Adventures of Robin Hood*: The Quintessential Children's Story." In *Touchstones: Reflections on the Best in Children's Literature*, vol. 2, ed. Perry Nodleman. West Lafayette, IN: Children's Literature Association, 1987: 213–220.
An overview of Pyle and his book in which Ranta argues that despite its difficulty, the book makes a good pedagogical tool, particularly for teaching children about the changing English language.

526. Rinetti, Carolyn. "*Beowulf*: Lessons from ORIAS Institute on History through Literature in the 6th/7th Grade Core Classrooms, 1998–2000." ED 463194.
This nine-page lesson plan is from the Office of Resources for International and Area Studies at the University of California at Berkeley.

Students compare the hero journey from other cultures with Beowulf's journey; they also evaluate historical evidence.

527. ———. "Marco Polo." ED 464844.
A two-day lesson plan for middle school students developed at the University of California at Berkeley's Summer Institute for Teachers on Cultural Interaction in the Medieval World. The document includes excerpts from "The Travels of Marco Polo" for students to read, as well as writing activities, lecture material, and detailed instructions for teachers.

528. *Scientia Scholae: A Journal for Teachers of Medieval Studies in Grades K–12.* http://www.teamsmedieval.org/scientia_scholae/
Published online twice a year, this journal is sponsored by TEAMS (see below under "Websites") and features articles and book reviews about the teaching of the Middle Ages. K–12 educators are encouraged to submit articles.

529. Self, David. "A Lost Asset? The Historical Novel in the Classroom." *Children's Literature in Education* 22 (1991): 45–49.
A British writer looks at the attitudes towards historical fiction in publishing and in education. He considers the work of Rosemary Sutcliff and other writers as he makes a case for the use of historical fiction in the classroom.

530. Shabbas, Audrey. "Living History with a Medieval Banquet in the Alhambra Palace." *Social Studies Review* 34.3 (Spring 1996): 22–29.
Middle school students learn about medieval Islamic civilization by putting on a banquet in which they assume the roles of possible guests.

531. Sipe, Lawrence R. "In Their Own Words: Authors' Views on Issues in Historical Fiction." *New Advocate* 10.3 (Summer 1997): 243–258.
Sipe examines the ideologies and attitudes of 19 children's writers who write historical fiction, finding that most are aware of both the didactic function of their work and the relationship between past and present. Sipe offers ideas for teachers who are using historical fiction, such as comparing documents the writers used as they crafted their fiction with the fiction itself, in order to help students understand the differences between history and fiction.

532. Smol, A. "Heroic Ideology and the Children's Beowulf." *Children's Literature* 22 (1994): 90–100.

In this scholarly article, Smol, a medievalist, looks at the ways Beowulf is presented—as a national hero and as a heroic model for boys—in late 19th- and early 20th-century children's versions of the poem.

533. *Studies in Medieval and Renaissance Teaching* (SMART).

Published twice a year at Wichita State University, *SMART* features articles about both the practical and philosophical side of teaching the Middle Ages and Renaissance to high school and college students (with an emphasis on the latter). Tables of contents of past issues—as well as ordering information—are available on the website, which is most easily accessed through the Labyrinth (see below under "Websites"), at http://www.georgetown.edu/labyrinth/professional/publishers/smart.html.

534. Talcroft, Barbara. *Death of the Corn King: King and Goddess in Rosemary Sutcliff's Historical Fiction for Young Adults*. Lanham, MD: Scarecrow, 1995.

In this reworking of her MA thesis, Talcroft discusses the way Sutcliff approaches religion in twelve of her novels, with chapters on the Celtic, Roman, Arthurian, and medieval books.

535. Trease, Geoffrey. "50 Years On: A Writer Looks Back." *Children's Literature in Education* 14 (Autumn 1983): 149–159.

In a self-deprecatory autobiographical essay, Trease discusses his first novel, *Bows against the Barons*, and the problems that now seem obvious with it, but which weren't when he was writing "at white heat, with a crude self-confidence it is now embarrassing to remember" (151). He goes on to consider his other novels and the social and literary context in which he wrote them.

536. ———. "The Historical Novelist at Work." *Children's Literature in Education* 7 (1972): 5–16.

Readers and writers of historical fiction are either fascinated by the differences between past and present—and thus approach fiction for escape—or they are drawn to the similarities between then and now, therefore reading to learn about humanity. Writers in the former camp write "costume novels"; the latter writers are more interested in characterization than costume, and write true historical fiction. Trease, of course, sets himself in the latter camp and discusses some of his novels, including *Mist over Athelney* (published in the U.S. as *Escape to King Alfred*), where the anti-immigrant bias of the Anglo-Saxons towards the Danes can be compared to the attitudes in England in the 1950s.

537. UCLA Lesson Plans.
These teacher resources, developed by the National Center for History in the Schools at the University of California at Los Angeles, describe activities based on primary sources. Each set of plans comes with a copy of the appropriate *Calliope* magazine (see above), although lesson plans are also available separately, and some are ERIC Documents. They can be purchased from Cobblestone Publishing at www.cobblestonepub.com. Subjects include: *The Byzantine Empire in the Age of Justinian* (Gr. 6+); *Coping with Catastrophe: The Black Death of the 14th Century* (Gr. 6+); *The Crusades from Medieval European and Muslim Perspectives* (Gr. 6+); *Ibn Battuta: A View of the 14th-Century World* (Gr. 7+).

538. Usrey, Malcolm. "A Milestone of Historical Fiction for Children: *Otto of the Silver Hand*." *Children's Literature Association Quarterly* 8.2 (Summer 1983): 25–26, 34.

539. Walsh, Jill Paton. "History Is Fiction." *Horn Book* 48 (1972): 17–23.
A writer defends historical novels against charges by historians that fact and fiction don't mix, and assertions by "believers in fiction" (17), who dislike the inclusion of history within fiction.

540. Webster, Armelle. "The Bayeux Tapestry: A Medieval Document Inspires Students." *Learning Languages* 1.2 (Winter 1996): 3–7.
A middle school teacher describes her research in France and England and how she incorporated it into lessons about the Bayeux Tapestry and the Norman Conquest.

541. Wintle, Justin, and Emma Fisher. *The Pied Pipers: Interviews with the Influential Creators of Children's Literature*. New York: Paddington Press, n.d.
Among the interviews presented here is one with Rosemary Sutcliff, in which she discusses her difficulty with writing about the later Middle Ages.

542. Woodard, Jo Ann A. "Medieval Universities: A Unit of Study for Grades 9–12." ED 376101. 1992.
A 66-page document from the National Center for History in the Schools, which is sponsored by the National Endowment for the Humanities. Students learn about the history and development of medieval universities in the 12th and 13th centuries, and how they fit into medieval society.

543. Zornado, Joseph. "A Poetics of History: Karen Cushman's Medieval World." *The Lion and the Unicorn* 21 (1997): 251–266.
Focusing not on the particulars of Cushman's novels but on interpreting them through the lens of Hayden White's *Metahistory: The Historical Imagination in Nineteenth-Century Europe*, Zornado discusses ideological readings of Cushman's work in this scholarly article.

Websites

Websites about the Middle Ages are ubiquitous; however, they vary enormously in quality. Several universities with the funds, the personnel, and the expertise to do so now sponsor websites maintained by scholars that include material for K–12 teachers and students. Also, many websites aimed at undergraduate college students have information, projects, and activities that can be modified for younger students. Three of the most important websites listed below are the Labyrinth, ORB, and NetSERF. Using their ever-expanding menus, students and teachers can find links to almost any kind of information about the Middle Ages, from online texts to manuscript images to sound files of medieval languages and music—and to lesson plans and teaching ideas. Many of the websites listed below are linked to each other. Of course, web addresses change quickly, but you can always use a search engine to find a title.

The Aberdeen Bestiary
http://www.abdn.ac.uk/bestiary/
This website is available as a link through the Labyrinth and other sources, but I list it here because it is one of the most appealing electronic sources dealing with manuscripts. The website reproduces the entire manuscript, with its fascinating images of real and imaginary an-

imals. The Latin text is transcribed and translated into English and a commentary is added. Students interested in medieval images will appreciate this website even if they never read any of the text. And those who want to research bestiaries will find plenty of information.

Anglo-Saxon Studies: A Select Bibliography
http://bubl.ac.uk/docs/bibliog/biggam/
C. P. Biggam, a British scholar, maintains this bibliography, which includes a section on children's books, both fiction and nonfiction, some with short annotations. This is a particularly useful source for finding British works about the Anglo-Saxons written in the 19th and early 20th centuries.

Arthuriana Pedagogy
http://www.smu.edu/arthuriana/teaching/index.html
Sponsored by *Arthuriana*, a scholarly journal published by the International Arthurian Society—North American Branch, this excellent website is for teachers at all levels, from preschool through graduate school. Lesson plans, classroom activities, syllabi, paper topics, project ideas, information about films, textbooks, and other websites—you can find all of that here. The site is maintained by Bonnie Wheeler of Southern Methodist University and Alan Baragona of the Virginia Military Institute.

The Camelot Project: Arthurian Texts, Images, Bibliographies, and Basic Information
http://www.lib.rochester.edu/camelot/cphome.stm
This is an excellent, authoritative resource for Arthurian literature. Maintained by Alan Lupack and Barbara Tepa Lupack at the Robbins Library, the University of Rochester, it provides information and links about Arthurian texts, characters, images, symbols, and more. It also gives bibliographies.

Castles of Wales
http://www.castlewales.com/home.html
Jeffrey L. Thomas is the editor, and both academic and nonacademic castle enthusiasts supply the photographs of (and a great deal of other information about) Welsh castles.

The Chaucer MetaPage
http://www.unc.edu/depts/chaucer/index.html
This clearinghouse for Chaucer web pages, maintained by scholars from
a group of institutions and housed at the University of North Carolina
at Chapel Hill, organizes and provides links to many of the best electronic resources about Chaucer's life and works. Teaching Chaucer at
all levels, from elementary through college, is one of the main features
of this website and it leads users to such resources as a guide to pro-
nouncing Chaucer. Its Meta-Mentors are retired professors who will an-
swer Chaucer questions; their e-mail addresses (as well as pictures and
short biographies) are included so students and teachers will have an
idea of who they are talking to.

*The Chaucer Pedagogy Page: Online Assistance for Teachers and Students
of Chaucer and the Later Middle Ages*
http://hosting/uaa.alaska.edu/afdtk/pedagogy.htm (Sometimes it's easier to access this one through the Chaucer MetaPage.)
Daniel T. Kline, an English professor at the University of Alaska at An-
chorage, maintains these helpful web pages. He includes ideas for
teaching Chaucer at all levels. In addition to background on Chaucer
and his times, K–12 assignments and research paper ideas are included.
And of course there are links to other good web pages.

The City of Women
http://library.thinkquest.org/12834/
Written by high school students Troy Scheid and Laura Troon, this
website is part of Thinkquest and shows the impressive kind of work
students can do. Although the site is not authoritative, it is very well-
designed and contains plenty of fascinating information, including biographies of medieval women and links to good sites, such as several on
costumes.

*EAWC: Exploring Ancient World Cultures: An Introduction to Ancient
and World Cultures on the World-Wide Web*
http://eawc.evansville.edu/mepage.htm
Edited by Anthony F. Beavers and maintained at the University of
Evansville (Indiana), this "on-line course supplement for teachers and
students of the ancient and medieval worlds" has a section on medieval

Europe. The site contains chapters of text introducing topics, plus links to texts (like "The Magna Carta") and scholarly articles. It also includes quizzes, images, essays, and Argos, a search engine designed to limit web searches to material about the ancient world. Aimed at college students, some of the information is accessible to younger students.

EDSITEment: The Best of the Humanities on the Web
http://www.edsitement.neh.gov/
Sponsored by the National Endowment for the Humanities, the National Trust for the Humanities, and the MarcoPolo Education Foundation, this wonderful website for teachers contains in-depth lesson plans and teaching materials. Lesson plans for medieval topics are available, including Dante, Chaucer, the Arthurian legend, and *Beowulf*, all for grades 9–12. Along with the plans, teachers can find downloadable handouts, links to other sites, and sound files.

Images of Medieval Art and Architecture
http://www.pitt.edu/~medart/
Alison Stones, an art history professor at the University of Pittsburgh, maintains this collection of images, organized by country, and featuring photos of castles, cathedrals, and stained glass. Scholarly bibliographies are also included.

Internet Medieval Sourcebook
http://www.fordham.edu/halsall/sbook1.html
Although the main audience is scholarly, this website, edited by Paul Halsall and maintained at Fordham University, offers online texts that may otherwise be hard to find, particularly on women's, Islamic, Byzantine, and Jewish history. Texts are presented both in abbreviated form for use in the classroom, and in full-text format.

The Labyrinth: Resources for Medieval Studies
http://www.georgetown.edu/labyrinth
All medieval disciplines are incorporated into this indispensable source, edited by scholars Martin Irvine and Deborah Everhart and maintained at Georgetown University. Although it was designed with academics in mind, it also includes information for K–12 teachers. Its vast menus carry links to databases, electronic texts, images, sounds, etc.

NetSERF: The Internet Connection for Medieval Resources
http://www.netserf.org/
This searchable clearinghouse of Internet medieval sources, edited by
Beau A. C. Harbin, has links to well over 1,700 sites, some scholarly,
some not. It also features news items about the Middle Ages, with links
to newspaper articles, and a glossary of 1,500 terms about the Middle
Ages.

Online Medieval and Classical Library
http://sunsite.berkeley.edu/OMACL/
Edited by Douglas B. Killings and maintained at the University of California at Berkeley, this is "a collection of some of the most important
literary works of Classical and Medieval civilization." Texts included
here are taken from older editions and translations of Norse sagas,
Arthurian works, Chaucer's poetry, etc. Most have a brief introduction
by Killings.

ORB: The Online Reference Book for Medieval Studies
http://www.the-orb.net/
This scholarly web page, maintained by Laura V. Blanchard and Carolyn Schriber, includes a useful encyclopedia, teaching resources, electronic texts, and helpful links to other sources.

*The Robin Hood Project, The University of Rochester (Texts, Images, Bib-
    liographies, and Basic Information)*
http://www.lib.rochester.edu/camelot/rh/rhhome/stm (Click on Re-
    lated Scholarly Projects and The Robin Hood Project to access this
    one.)
Like the Camelot Project, this site was designed and is maintained by
Alan Lupack and Barbara Tepa Lupack of the Robbins Library at the
University of Rochester. Its bibliographies are aimed at a scholarly audience, but its links to other Robin Hood websites, its online texts of
ballads, its images of Robin Hood over the centuries, and its filmography will be useful to anyone interested in the topic.

TEAMS, The Consortium for the Teaching of the Middle Ages
www.teamsmedieval.org
Founded by the Medieval Academy of America, TEAMS is now an independent nonprofit educational corporation whose goal is to support

the teaching of the Middle Ages at all levels, from elementary through college. Links on its website include teaching resources, online texts, and announcements of National Endowment for the Humanities Summer Seminars and Institutes for High School Teachers (those with medieval themes). It also includes a link to the online journal *Scientia Scholae: A Journal for Teachers of Medieval Studies in Grades K–12* (see above, under "Periodicals").

What Was It Really Like to Live in the Middle Ages?
http://www.learner.org/exhibits/middleages/
This website is part of the Annenberg Foundation and the Corporation for Public Broadcasting's joint project dedicated to excellence in teaching. The project incorporates videos and print material in addition to its well-organized, easy-to-use website, which includes the Middle Ages among many other topics. The website is written at a middle school level and gives an overview of life in the high Middle Ages. Links to other websites, interactive questions, and suggestions for projects are included. For example, students can look at images of a medieval tapestry, read stories other students have written about it, write their own stories, and visit other links about tapestries.

CHAPTER FIFTEEN

Classroom Activities

Many of the books, articles, and websites listed in the previous chapter are full of teaching ideas, and activities for students studying the Middle Ages appear in several of the works cited in other chapters (see "activities" in the subject index for a complete list). In this chapter, I offer a few more ways to allow students to explore the medieval world.

Teachers might help their students to understand the vast gulf between manuscript and print cultures in a number of ways. Runic inscription, manuscript, and calligraphy projects can combine art, language, and historical research. Creative writing is another excellent way to help students understand the details of the medieval period. As they write, students conduct research in order to present their subjects accurately. And finally, students can learn about the ways medieval people viewed the world by trying science and math projects.

Runic Inscriptions

Many books about the Vikings include the Futhark (or Futhork), the runic alphabet, which was also known and used in Anglo-Saxon England. For example, "The Rune Poem" uses runes within its text, and the poet Cynewulf signed his name in some of his poems by using runes. Runes can convey both alphabetic symbols and words (e.g., *wynn*, the *w* rune, which looks like a modern *P*, is also the Anglo-Saxon word for "joy"). Although many books about the Vikings include the Futhark, *Runes* by R. I. V. Page (Reading the Past Series, University of California / British Museum, 1988) is an excellent source for understanding runes.

- Students can write their own messages using runes, and then interpret each other's messages. In a more ambitious project, they can carve or burn them into wood.
- Fans of *The Lord of the Rings* can compare J. R. R. Tolkien's runic alphabet, the Angerthas (found in the appendix to the third volume of the trilogy) with the Futhark. Have them describe the ways Tolkien uses his runes on the title pages of the books, or on the inscription on Balin's tomb, in *The Fellowship of the Ring* (book II, chapter 4).

The Classroom Scriptorium

Medieval Calligraphy

While studying manuscript facsimiles on the web or in the numerous books available from libraries, students can practice their own calligraphy. Marc Drogin's *Yours Truly, King Arthur: How Medieval People Wrote, and How You Can, Too* (entry 100), along with other books about the how-tos of medieval calligraphy and illumination, will help. To imitate the flat-edged nib calligraphers used, and to avoid the mess of ink, students only need two pencils and two rubber bands. Rubber-banding the pencils side by side, with the points held evenly on the page, simulates a flat-edged nib and gives students a tool with which to practice lettering. Medieval alphabets can be found in many calligraphy books, including Drogin's, and in books written for adults, such as Stan Knight's *Historical Scripts: A Handbook for Calligraphers* (London: Adam and Charles Black, 1984) or *The Historical Source Book for Scribes* (University of Toronto Press, 1999) by Michelle P. Brown and Patricia Lovett. Students can practice composing and writing their own messages, perhaps becoming King Alfred's scribe as he composes a message to an abbot about the Danish invasions, or writing a message from Guenevere to Lancelot.

To take this project further, a class could be divided up into the various practitioners needed in the scriptorium. One person might rule the page, another write the text, and a third illuminate the opening initial, while others proofread and correct it, or bind the pages into booklets. Christopher de Hamel's *Scribes and Illuminators* (University of Toronto Press, 1992), while not an instruction book, provides fascinating information that would be useful here, as does Michelle P. Brown's *The British Library Guide to Writing and Scripts* (University of Toronto Press, 1998).

Chaucer Manuscripts
Facsimiles of Chaucer manuscripts can be challenging to decipher, but they provide a welcome puzzle for visual and detail-oriented students. Using a manuscript page from *The Canterbury Tales*, along with a copy of a Middle English version of the text, students can transcribe the text letter by letter, determining where the printed text differs. Are the spellings the same? Does the manuscript's scribe use abbreviations? What about punctuation—do you see question marks, periods, commas, or exclamation marks? A CD-ROM of one of the two most complete versions of *The Canterbury Tales* is available that allows students to look at the manuscript and a transcription of it side by side: *The Hengwrt Chaucer*, edited by Ceridwen Lloyd-Morgan (Scholarly Digital Editions, www.sd-editions.com). Also, many college and university libraries own inexpensive facsimiles of Chaucer manuscripts, and single pages are available online.

A Latin Psalter
Many manuscripts were written in Latin, a language a scribe might not necessarily know, particularly in the later Middle Ages, when manuscripts were no longer made just in nunneries and monasteries. Some scribes copied manuscripts letter by letter, not sure of the words they were writing. Look at the page from a 14th-century French psalter on the cover of this book. Have students try to copy a line from it. What differences do they see between the way the letters are formed here and the way they have been taught to write? Look particularly at the letter *s*, which is shaped more like an *f*, in the word *sicut* (line 3). But compare that with the first word in the last line, *adusus* (an abbreviation for

adversus). Notice how an *s* at the end of a word looks like our *s*. Also notice that the scribe uses a *u* to indicate a *v* here, but not in the gold letter that begins line 3.

Many of the letters on the page are formed from the *i*-like stroke called a minim, including *u*, *m*, *n*, and *i* itself. Consider the amount of confusion this can cause, especially for people who don't know Latin very well. Have students think up as many combinations of the letters made of minims as they can (including the word *minim*, which is a combination of ten minims). For example, in the very first word on the manuscript page, what are the possible combinations of letters after the *f* and before the *d*? In actuality, the letters are *un*, but they could be *iin*, *mi*, *im*, *nn*, *uu*, *ini*, *iui*, etc. And the scribal practice of using *u* instead of *v* makes even more minim confusion.

Compare the psalter page with a modern Bible page from Psalms. Have students list as many differences as they can between the two, including the layout, the punctuation, the decoration, the dotting of *i*'s, even the number of words on a line. Modern Bibles include chapter and verse numbers, but medieval Bibles did not. What other differences can students find? Then have them compare these Bibles with an early printed one, for example, the Gutenberg page reproduced in Fisher (entry 339). Does the Gutenberg page look more like a manuscript or a printed book?

The psalter page is decorated with red and blue pigment, as well as gold leaf. The small *v* that begins line 3, the large *D* that begins line 7, and a few other letters have been illuminated with gold. You can also see the shadow of the writing and decorations from the other side of the page, particularly on the right-hand side.

The text on this page comes from Psalms 82–83 (Vulgate 81–82). Below is a transcription of the first six lines, the end of Psalm 82. The endings of some words are abbreviated—for example, the odd symbol following the *b* at the end of both of the middle words in line 6 stands for *-us*. In the transcription, the italicized letters are expansions of the abbreviations. We abbreviate words in a similar way, writing *w/* to mean *with* or *b/c* to mean *because*, and using a variety of signs to mean *and*. However, we rarely use such abbreviations in formal writing. Have students think about why the scribe of such an expensive manuscript, decorated with gold, would use abbreviations.

1. fundamenta terre.
2. Ego dixi dii estis: *et* filii excelsi omnes.
3. Vos autem sicut homines mouemini
4. *et* sicut unus de principib*us* cadetis.
5. Surge deus iudica terram. q*uonia*m tu here
6. ditabis in omnibus gentibus. Psalmus

Here is how the lines are translated in the Douay edition of the Bible, which is very close to the Latin: "foundations of the earth. I have said: you are gods and all of you the sons of the Most High. But you like men shall die: and shall fall like one of the princes. Arise, O God, judge thou the earth: for thou shalt inherit among all the nations." Line 6 ends with the word "psalmus," written in red, showing that one psalm is ending and another is beginning. The scribe seems to have made an error in the last word of line 3, which should read *moriemini*, "you shall die," not *mouemini*. He probably confused the minims in the book he was copying from, since in his alphabet, *r* can look a lot like *i*.

Below is a transcription and a translation of the rest of the page, beginning with the large gold *D*, the opening of Psalm 83.

7. Deus quis similis erit tibi ne ta
8. ceas neq*ue* compescaris deus.
9. Q*uonia*m ecce inimici tui sonauerunt. *et* qu*i*
10. oderunt te extulerunt caput
11. Super po*pulum* tuum malignauerunt
12. consilium. *et* cogitauerunt aduersus sa*n*
13. ctos tuos.
14. Dixerunt uenite *et* disperdamus eos de
15. gente. *et* non memoretur nomen isr*a*hel ultr*a*
16. Q*uonia*m cogitauerunt unanimiter sim*ul*
17. adu*er*sus te testamentum disposuerunt.

The Douay translation reads, "O God, who shall be like to thee? Hold not thy peace, neither be thou still, O God. For lo, thy enemies have made a noise: and they that hate thee have lifted up the head. They have taken a malicious counsel against thy people, and have consulted against thy saints. They have said: Come and let us destroy them, so that they be not a nation: and let the name of Israel be remembered no more. For they have contrived with one consent: they have made a covenant together against thee."

Notice the way words are sometimes begun on one line and finished on the next. For example, the last word in line 7 is *taceas*, but only the *ta* appears on that line. Line 12 ends with *sanctos*, but again, only the first syllable is on line 12 (the *n* is indicated by the line over the *a*.) Compare modern practices for dividing words with medieval practices.

Editing Manuscripts

Advanced students might try their hands at editing a manuscript passage. For teachers, the challenge is finding an appropriate manuscript facsimile, yet they do exist, and resources such as Jackdaws provide reproducible material (see entry 504). High school students who have already looked at some examples of Old and Middle English and who have a little background in the history of the English language can learn more by seeing what kinds of work editors do when they prepare medieval texts to be presented in textbooks. These students might prepare an edition of a late Middle English text, adding explanatory footnotes about both language and historical background, deciding what abbreviations need to be expanded, and what archaic spellings need to be modernized. Or they might prepare a modernization of the text, using Modern English syntax and spelling. My article "Students Editing Manuscripts," *Studies in Medieval and Renaissance Teaching* 7.2 (Fall 1999): 17–21, gives a detailed description of this project.

Creative Writing in the Classroom

A Day in the Life of . . .

Alun Hicks and Dave Martin give plenty of suggestions for teaching history through the writing of fiction (see entries 499–500). A similar project is to have students write "A Day in the Life of . . ." stories. Choosing a real or imaginary person from the time period being studied, students research the details of daily life in order to portray a day, from sunup to sundown, of Eleanor of Aquitaine, or a page in a 12th-century French castle, or an ale brewer in a small village in 14th-century England.

In a variation on this project students might write an autobiography of a longer period in the life of a fictional person from the medieval period, again incorporating details from research to make the life story plausible and convincing.

The greatest challenge in these types of projects is not the incorporation of physical details but the portrayal of the mind-set of a person from a vastly different culture from ours, with different ideas about religion, gender, social equality, and tolerance for difference. Merely setting a modern character into a setting with the physical attributes of a historical period does not lead to an understanding of that time period.

Medieval Mysteries

In another creative writing project, students decide on a probable solution to an unsolved medieval mystery. They include their solutions within stories they write. For example, when Margery Kempe, the 15th-century English mystic, was a young woman, she became so ill that everyone thought she would die. The priest was sent for so she could say her final confession, but he was so harsh with her that she never told him about a certain terrible sin that she had committed, a sin she thought would keep her from heaven. In her autobiography, she tells this story, but she never reveals what the sin was. High school students might read the beginning of her book in Barry Windeatt's translation, *The Book of Margery Kempe* (Penguin, 1985), and write their own versions of her sin.

Another mystery involves the works of Geoffrey Chaucer. In his "Retractions," Chaucer lists the works he has written, including "The Book of the Lion," which is unknown to us. Using what they know of Chaucer's other works, students might speculate on, or write their own lines from this lost work.

From the Anglo-Saxon period comes another literary mystery. King Alfred the Great kept a little book, his "Enchiridion," with him all the time to copy passages important to him. Asser, one of his priests, mentions it in his biography of Alfred, conveniently reproduced in Michael Lapidge's *Alfred the Great* (Penguin, 1988). Students can look through texts surviving from Anglo-Saxon England, including saints' lives, maxims, poetry, and biblical passages, to speculate on what King Alfred's "Enchiridion" might have contained.

Finally, students might look into the mystery of the English princes who may or may not have been murdered by Richard III during the Hundred Years' War. William Lace's book (entry 250) would be a good starting point to speculate on what happened to Crown Prince Edward and his brother.

Riddles

Medieval people enjoyed riddles, and many Anglo-Saxon riddles were preserved in the tenth-century manuscript *The Exeter Book*. Kevin Crossley-Holland has translated some of them in his *Exeter Book Riddles* (Penguin Classics, 1993), and in *The New Exeter Book Riddles* (Enitharmon Press, 2000); many other translations are also available. Compare Crossley-Holland's translations with those of other writers. Which ones use Anglo-Saxon poetic devices like alliteration and kennings? Which do you prefer, and why? Students might work in groups to solve some Anglo-Saxon riddles before writing their own and exchanging them with other groups to see if they have provided enough clues to allow readers to find the answers. They might incorporate Anglo-Saxon poetic devices like alliteration and caesuras in each line, or compounds and kennings.

Continuing the Story

In his poetic drama "The Homecoming of Beorhtnoth Beorhthelm's Son," J. R. R. Tolkien writes a verse drama in which he continues the events in the Old English poem "The Battle of Maldon" (the text is reprinted in *The Tolkien Reader* [Ballantine, 1966]). Students might continue a different part of "The Battle of Maldon" or another poem in the same vein, perhaps imitating Old English poetic forms and language to tell the story of the men who fled the battle, or telling the story of the slave who uncovered the dragon's hoard in *Beowulf*. Or they might tell one of *The Canterbury Tales* from the point of view of another character; John the Carpenter might have a very different idea about the events that led him to string those tubs up under the roof in "The Miller's Tale," for example.

Science and Math

Medieval Measurements

In the medieval period measuring was sometimes done using the hypsometer, a geometric device that's easy to make. Students consult a book like E. Richard Churchill's *Paper Science Toys* (Sterling, 1990) to learn how to construct your own hypsometer and measure the height of a nearby building.

Medieval Math

Arabic numbers did not become common in Western Europe until the later Middle Ages—and in England, not until the 1600s. Furthermore, the concept of zero, while used in India and the Arab world, was not widely accepted in the medieval West until the 15th century. Even when Arabic numerals began to be used on a limited basis in Western Europe, they didn't always look like the forms we are familiar with, as Marc Drogin shows in *Medieval Calligraphy: Its History and Technique* (Dover, 1980, p. 170).

The most common Roman numerals are I (1), V (5), X (10), L (50), C (100), D (500), and M (1000). Have students try doing some simple math problems using only Roman numerals. Can they do so without converting them to Arabic numerals in their heads?

The Shape of the Universe

Very few medieval people thought the earth was flat. Educated people, and especially those interested in science, knew it was round. Nevertheless, their astronomy was very different from ours. Scholars who read Ptolemy's *Almagest*, or who studied Aristotle's views, believed the earth was at the center of the universe. Students may research the Ptolemaic idea of the universe. Then they might find out about Copernicus's 16th-century theories: in the Copernican view, the earth revolves around the sun. Have students draw models of these two visions of the universe and write two different paragraphs explaining what they see every day when the sun, the moon, and the stars rise and set. In one paragraph, they should take the Ptolemaic, geocentric view, in the other, a Copernican, heliocentric stance.

APPENDIX

Not the Middle Ages

The following books are often said to be historical fiction with medieval settings. In bibliographies, in reviews, in textbooks, on websites, and in journal articles, books that take place in a preindustrial setting, or a social setting with a strict hierarchy of classes, are frequently classified as historical fiction about the Middle Ages, as each of the following has been at some point. Although some of the authors do draw on the medieval period for settings or details, none of the following books is historical fiction about the Middle Ages.

544. Fleischman, Sid. *The Whipping Boy*. Illus. Peter Sis. New York: Greenwillow, 1986. 90 pp. (0-688-06216-4 hc.) Middle.
This delightful story of the adventures a bratty prince and his whipping boy encounter when they run away from the castle has elements of the Middle Ages—as well as the Renaissance, the 18th, and even the 19th century, but it's set in none of them. Fleischman is telling an adventure story, not writing a historical novel. A castle and knights might make the book seem medieval, but there are also powdered wigs, potatoes, and umbrellas, none of which belong to the medieval period.

545. Fox, Paula. *The King's Falcon*. Illus Eros Keith. Englewood Cliffs, NJ: Bradbury Press, 1969. 56 pp. Elementary-Middle.

The sad, philosophical king of a tiny, fictional kingdom that is really ruled by the domineering queen finds happiness only in helping the falconer catch and train a young falcon. Finally, he decides to leave his kingdom to find a position as a falconer. Keith's two-color wash and ink drawings fit the somber tone of this story which incorporates medieval motifs into its telling, but which tells readers little about the real Middle Ages.

546. Gerrard, Roy. *Sir Cedric*. New York: Farrar, Straus & Giroux, 1984. 32 pp. (0-374-36953 hc.) Elementary.
In galloping rhymes and cartoon-like paintings, tiny, dwarf-like Sir Cedric leaves his castle for some adventure. He rescues Fat Matilda, a princess, and fights Black Ned, a villain. Elements of chivalry give the book a medieval flavor, but Gerrard's intent is to have fun, not to present an accurate view of the Middle Ages.

547. ———. *Sir Cedric Rides Again*. New York: Farrar, Straus & Giroux, 1986. 32 pp. (0-606-13775-0 hc.) Elementary.
Sir Cedric is back, with his impossible daughter Edwina and her suitor, Hubert the Hopeless. They journey from England to Palestine, where Edwina and her mother are kidnapped by Abdul the infidel, who looks more like Jabba the Hut than the Palestinian bandit he is supposed to be—but like the first volume, this book isn't really about the medieval period; it just uses castles and knights and armor for atmosphere.

548. Jordan, Sherryl. *The Raging Quiet*. New York: Simon and Schuster, 1999. 266 pp. (0-689-82140-9 hc.) Junior.
An agricultural economy, manor houses, priests, peasants, and accusations of witchcraft make this tale of a young woman learning to communicate with a deaf boy (who is considered by villagers to be mad) appear at first glance to have a medieval setting. However, in her author's note, Jordan remarks that she "could not force [the story] into a particular time or place in history." She says she "left [the] tale in the freer atmosphere of myth, and simply wrote a fantasy set in an ancient time" (265).

549. McKinley, Robin. *The Hero and the Crown*. 1984. New York: Berkley Books, 1986. 227 pp. (0-688-02593-5 pb.) Junior-Senior.

This Newbery Medal–winning fantasy takes place in the mythical land of Damar and includes talking, fire-breathing dragons. It's a rich and wonderful book, but historical fiction it is not.

550. Pierce, Tamora. *Alanna: The First Adventure*. New York: Random House, 1983. 230 pp. (0-679-80114-6 pb.) Middle-Junior.

Like the other books in the Song of the Lioness Quartet, and, indeed, in Pierce's other quartets, this is a fantasy, as is clear from the map of the Kingdom of Tortall in the beginning of the book. The book uses information about medieval European military training as Alanna works her way to becoming a knight, but Pierce makes no attempt to write historical fiction; she writes fantasy.

551. Voigt, Cynthia. *Jackaroo*. New York: Scholastic Point. 292 pp. (0-590-48595-4 pb.) Junior-Senior.

In her impressive and complex tale of a young peasant woman who longs for justice, Voigt uses elements of medieval Europe. But the geography of her Kingdom is her own invention, and many other aspects of life in the Kingdom do not reflect medieval society, most tellingly the absence of Christianity. Further, the Kingdom's lower classes are forbidden to read, but no such prohibition was placed on the medieval peasantry.

Index

Authors

Note: Numbers refer to entries, not pages. Only authors of works for young readers are included. Entries from chapter 14, "Professional Resources for Educators," are included when they refer to works for young readers.

Titles

Subjects

Norman Conquest, 214, 215, 219, 217,
221, 224, 225, 231, 232, 246, 379,
504, 540
Norman England, 009, 072, 243, 246
Norse mythology, 435, 449, 486

Patrick, St., 206
Peasants' Revolt, 256, 289, 504
Peterborough Chronicle, 266
Pied Piper of Hamelin, 358, 368, 428,
441
pilgrimage, 020, 103, 110, 265, 300
plague, 051, 112–117, 276, 288, 289,
306, 345, 348, 486, 504, 537
printing, 334, 270
Ptolemaic Universe, 001

recipes, 013, 016, 031, 033, 066, 054,
159
Reynard the Fox, 427, 429, 439
Richard I (Lionheart), 022, 077, 324,
386, 394, 418
Richard II, 284
Richard III, 250
Robert the Bruce, 275, 277, 314
Robin Hood, 245, 321–332, 437, 448,
479, 483, 488, 506, 509, 524, 525

Saladin, 077, 390, 418
Song of Roland, 217, 300, 434, 437,
448, 455, 456, 477, 521
Spens, Sir Patrick, 274
Stephen (king of England), 266

tools, 008, 041, 046, 049, 097, 104,
147, 156
troubadours. See minstrels and
troubadours

universities, 040, 273, 367, 542

Varangian Guard, 192, 197, 198, 200,
425
Vikings in Ireland, 184, 189, 190, 204,
209, 210, 211
Vikings in North America, 142, 143,
146, 151, 152, 154, 155, 163, 170,
173, 174, 187, 202, 203

Wallace, William, 275, 277
Whittington, Dick, 272
William the Conqueror, 022, 215, 219,
224, 232, 247, 379
women, 018, 021, 046, 053, 056, 501

Locations

British Isles: Vikings in, 170, 194, 199,
201
Byzantium, 005, 008–010, 053, 123,
125, 128, 197, 200, 412, 422, 425,
426, 486, 504, 537

China, 411, 413-417, 421
Constantinople [modern Istanbul,
Turkey], 192, 198, 233, 377, 422,
425, 486

Denmark, 176, 177, 179, 190, 233;
Hedeby, 141

Egypt, 359, 388, 418
England, 048–050, 090, 108, 109, 173,
206, 233, 237–333, 335, 340, 341,
356, 382, 386, 388, 426, 432–434,
437, 438, 444, 448, 451, 454,
457–462, 467, 469, 486, 504;
Canterbury, 225, 236, 244, 251,
255, 309, 319; Cornwall, 264;
Cotswolds, 271; Durham, 106;
Glastonbury, 278; Hastings, 214,
215, 219, 221, 224, 225, 231, 235;
Horsted, 219; Isle of Wight, 091;

About the Author

Before **Rebecca Barnhouse** earned her doctorate in medieval literature from the University of North Carolina at Chapel Hill, she taught high school English. Now she teaches literature and writing courses at Youngstown State University, where she is involved in outreach programs in the local public schools. Her publications include *Recasting the Past: The Middle Ages in Young Adult Literature*, and she edits *The LYRE Review*, an online review journal written for and by young readers (www.cc.ysu.edu/lyre).